decoding
your destiny

10664149

decoding
your destiny

Carmen Harra, Ph.D.

BEYOND
WORDS
Publishing
I N C

Beyond Words Publishing, Inc.
20827 N.W. Cornell Road, Suite 500
Hillsboro, Oregon 97124-9808
503-531-8700
503-531-8773 fax

Editor: Julie Steigerwaldt
Managing editor: Henry Covey
Proofreaders: Jade Chan and Marvin Moore
Author photograph: © 2003 Josh Gosfield
Cover and interior design: Carol Sibley
Composition: William H. Brunson Typography Services

Printed in the United States of America

ISBN-13: 978-1-58270-143-1
ISBN-10: 1-58270-143-1

The corporate mission of Beyond Words Publishing, Inc.:
Inspire to Integrity

I offer you peace.
I offer you love.
I offer you friendship.
I see your beauty. I hear your need.
I feel your feelings.
My wisdom flows from the Highest Source.
I salute that Source in you.
Let us work together for unity and love.

MAHATMA GANDHI, *Prayer for Peace*

CONTENTS

Acknowledgments

This book was written with the help of the Invisible World and the power of the Divine energy. My beautiful parents, Alexandrina and Victor Muresan, and my grandfather, Octavian Goga, told me about this book years ago. From the valley of the eternity they guided me into it. I am so grateful for all their help.

I am thankful for the inspiration that came from all the people in my amazing family: my daughters, Alexandra, Florina, and Carmen; my husband, Virgil; my sister, Mona; and my grandchildren, Esmeralda, Anthony, and Francisco. I am also grateful to Allie Swain Muresan and Silviu Sotea for all their love and help.

I also want to thank all my great friends: Maureen O'Neil, William Norwich, Victoria Holt, Arielle Ford, Cornelia Guest, Doug Warner, Joe Esposito, and Dennis O'Connel, and the thousands of my wonderful clients and patients. They have taught me about compassion, patience, wisdom, religion, acceptance, love, and peace.

I want to thank Mary Hebert for her help and her great spirit.

I also want to express my love and gratitude to my superb publishers, Cynthia Black and Richard Cohn, my wonderful publicist, Bridget O'Brien, and my editor, Julie Steigerwaldt, for making this project possible.

I thank all the teachers of the world for allowing me to connect with the perfect coded language of the Universe.

This book is about survival, transformation, and understanding the future. The world will see the light of the Divine Absolute to reach Nirvana.

What lies behind us
and what lies before us
are tiny matters
compared to what lies within us.

OLIVER W. HOLMES

No pessimist ever discovered the secrets of stars,
or sailed to an uncharted land, or opened a
new doorway for the human spirit.

HELEN KELLER

All my life I've listened to my inner voice, telling me where
to go and what to do. That inner voice was a constant

source of comfort and gave me the confidence to follow my path with complete awareness. The more I listened, the stronger it became and the more I trusted what I heard. To me, that voice comes from the right side of the brain and is all-knowing. That's the side of the brain I can trust because it was "programmed" by my agreements, my soul's "contract" that I signed before I was born.

Each of us has made an agreement to be here, and that agreement is coded within us. When we listen to our inner knowledge, the path to keeping those agreements and fulfilling our life's purpose is revealed to us. As amazing as that sounds, I am living proof, and so are the many people who have worked with me. Their stories appear in this book. In my life, I have had only one choice: to believe what my inner voice was telling me. As Robert Frost wrote in his famous poem, "The Road Not Taken," that choice has "made all the difference."

I was born behind the Iron Curtain during one of the most oppressive Communist regimes in Romanian history, under Ceausescu. Basic human rights did not exist, and neither did freedom of speech or the right to travel. Armed guards patrolled the streets and borders. There was very little food. Buying a quart of milk meant standing in line for ten hours and hoping there would be some left when your turn came. People died from hunger. Life was without hope. Everyone wanted to escape.

I remember being young and feeling as though I were living inside a prison. Yet I could see my future, and it looked very different from the reality I was living. I believed in myself and trusted what my inner voice was telling me every step of the way. My need to know more about myself was strong. By nature I had a happy disposition. I stayed on the brighter side of my visions and worked to attract the good. I sometimes wonder what my life would have been like if I had remained in fear, if I had failed to act fearlessly about my future.

Ultimately I was successful in Romania. My career as a singer had made me famous by the time I was sixteen. As a celebrity I had privileges. I had money, a house, and a car. For that part of the world, I had a good life. Then one day I knew my time there was over. Even though it meant leaving behind everything I had, I knew another life was waiting for me.

The future should always bring something new and exciting. When I arrived in America in my twenties, my pockets were empty. I had no place to live. I spoke English poorly. I had nothing except my belief in myself. Here I am today, with a successful career and a jewelry business, writing a second book in a language that at one time I did not know!

My friend Lynne once told me that I chose a difficult path to show others that anything is possible when we listen to our higher awareness. For me, staying in Romania would have meant a life of stagnation; I never would have accomplished the work I was meant to do. It was my karma to be born in Romania into an oppressive Communist regime, but it was within my soul code to overcome obstacles by using my gifts to help myself and, ultimately, others. And it was through the actions of my free will that I took responsibility for my life and altered the course of my destiny.

When I was eleven years old I lived in Bistrita, a town in northern Transylvania. One day I went to the theater to see a new American movie featuring a young actress named Candice Bergen. When I got home, I told my parents that I would meet her someday. Years later when I came to the United States, she was the first celebrity I met! My conviction in my vision had made it happen. At the time, I had no way of knowing anything about her or how to contact her. I knew it was my fate, so it was in my hands to see my destiny fulfilled.

Prediction empowers the mind. Throughout my life, I've put tremendous faith in my predictions. I focus on projecting a positive outcome whenever possible. I've predicted my career, my marriage, and my lifestyle. My predictions come from my own inner guidance. But sometimes the messages I receive are confirmed by all the angels around me—especially my grandfather, mother, and father.

I adored my father. He died many years ago in Romania, but I still talk to him every day. Before he died, he told me several things that I will never forget. One day he said, "Carmen, you will leave this country when the time is right. We have something else to accomplish." Years later when I was ready to leave Romania, his words helped me to trust that I was doing the right thing. My father never presented himself as psychic or special. He loved life deeply and believed what he felt in his heart. He's helped me do the same.

My mother was a great psychic without realizing it. So many things she told me have come true. One day she said to me, "Your father and I are not going to live for very long, and you have to accept that. You will live longer than we will. I will die very soon, Carmen." Then she never mentioned it again. I didn't want to believe her. I told her she wasn't dying. Two months later, she passed away. My intuition didn't work when it came to my mother's death because I didn't want her to go.

Losing my mother was a major turning point in my life. We all go through times of major loss or change, but how we deal with these events and lessons depends on our belief system and where we are in our awareness. Predictions can also give us a way to explore future possibilities in preparation for these major life changes.

By nature we are afraid to know our future. Instead we take things as they come and avoid interfering with destiny. *Que sera sera!* We go through life believing, "It's better to not know," or "Whatever is meant to happen will happen." We believe life is unpredictable because we have not dared to imagine how predictable life can be! The people who succeed in life are those who are confident and in tune with themselves. They build their lives consciously, which takes a strong will. Knowledge is the power that leads to accomplishment. If you don't know yourself, your abilities, and your potential, your wishes will never come true.

By the time I was a teenager, I already knew that I would have a career in music and that I would move to another part of the world. I was also told about my book and whom I would marry. It's possible to miss vital information if you are not listening and not working on your future. It's important to know where you are going. Because I knew what direction I was headed in, I took the appropriate initiatives; I acted as if the predictions were already true.

When I was younger, I kept a notebook of all my predictions. Reading them years later, I was surprised that almost everything had come true. One of my predictions was that I would have my own television talk show. The only other information I received was that I would be doing the show with a woman named Victoria. In 1998 I met a producer named Victoria. I knew that she was not the Victoria in my prediction, but I felt a strong connection with her. After my first book was published, I received a call from her asking me to come to Los Angeles to work on a television show. We did the pilot, but nothing came of it.

Then in December 2003, I went to Puerto Rico for a conference with the Alliance for the New Humanity. I was looking forward to being with Deepak Chopra and Al Gore and participating in discussions about the future of the world, but I also knew that someone I was meant to meet would be there.

Sure enough, at one of the seminars, a woman introduced herself to me: "My name is Victoria Holt, and I'd love to talk about the Divine Feminine Energy." I knew she was the reason I was there. I gave her my book and my business card. She thanked me and then apologized, saying she was so overwhelmed that she had no time to talk with me.

Three days later, back home in Florida, my cell phone rang. It was Victoria, thanking me for writing *Everyday Karma*. "I'd love to do a show called *Everyday Karma* with you," she said. Three months later the pilot was ready, and it has recently been pitched to ABC. Another show I'm involved in, *The Gift*, has just been sold to the SciFi Channel.

As I interpret Einstein's theory of relativity, everything is possible. The concept of relativity means that when you shift your thinking, you shift the quantum and physical world around you. Physical reality is not fixed; everything depends on everything else. Thus, in a relative world, the realm of possible outcomes is infinite! The law of quantum physics tells us that we live in the past, present, and future simultaneously and that energy moves from the past to the present and to the future at the speed of light. That explains why we have so many premonitions and why feelings of déjà vu are so intense within our conscious reality.

To predict, you have to set your mind in motion. When I met Dennis O'Connel, I told him that we would be doing business together one day. Some time later, after an article about me appeared in the *New York Times*, Judy Gordon, a producer at the *Today* show, came to see me and put me in touch with Janet, the owner of Fragments, a production company that specializes in jewelry. Janet then introduced me to QVC, the TV shopping network. Four years later, Dennis became my assistant and one of the designers of my jewelry line on QVC.

In life you have to pay attention to the signs. Signs can come in the form of symbols such as numbers, names, colors, or other forms of energy. If you pay attention, you will notice that some names or initials come into your life over and over again. For instance, my first agent was named Janise; my music producer was Janet; the woman who helped get my jewelry line on QVC was also named Janet; the buyer at QVC who gave me the contract is named Jeannie; and my other jewelry designer is Joe!

Letters, like numbers, carry vibrations and resonance. Repetition of names or first initials is a sign of synchronicity in our lives. It shows that we are attracting people of similar vibrations, hopefully to help us. It is confirmation that we are listening and on the right path.

In moments of sadness and desperation, I rely on the fact that there is always tomorrow—the future. As long as we believe in the laws of transformation, we can turn anything around. Even the darkest episode in our life can be a door to evolution. Giving in to stagnation and darkness is giving in to fear. And it is this fear that blocks our perception, our ability to see differently and to project a different future.

Here on Earth we are all in the School of Life. It's not always easy. It requires learning and changing. Often we are all reluctant to change, but our willingness to change is what opens the door to our future self.

There is a big difference between chance, possibility, and what is meant to be. If you're meant to be a famous personality, you will get there no matter what—that's your destiny. But how you will deal with your fame is up to you. That's your free will. Free will interferes with destiny.

Everything is connected in the process of becoming, of what is meant to be. When we live with that awareness—that there is a reason for everything that happens to us—we begin to move through life differently, with more trust, more gratitude—and more excitement.

Whatever your reason for choosing to read this book, may it inspire you to remember the magnificent being you are.

INTRODUCTION

Was Princess Diana meant to die so young? Was September 11 predicted before it happened? Is the melting of the polar icecaps inevitable? Was the pope meant to die after Easter during the "Week of the Light"? What is destined to be and what is not? How much can we know about our future, and how can we control our destiny?

In this book, you will learn how the physical world is made up of codes and how these codes reveal what is in store for us. Da Vinci has a code; Nostradamus has a code; even the Bible and the Great Pyramid have codes. These numeric codes can be calculated and were used by the prophets, along with astrological readings, to make predictions.

You, too, have codes—a soul code and a genetic code. Understanding the meaning behind your soul code is the key to your destiny—to knowing who you are and what lessons you are meant to learn in this life.

In my first book, *Everyday Karma*, I shared my personal experiences as well as a ten-step program for resolving your karma. In *Decoding Your Destiny*, I go a step further and show that once you have resolved your karma, you are ready to shape your own future. Knowledge is power. Knowing your true self, by decoding your destiny, enables you to make the choices that will serve your highest good and make the most of what was meant to be.

In this book you will learn how to calculate your own soul code—your particular vibration and rhythm—to reveal the unique skills and abilities you were born with and the path of your soul's evolution. But once you have decoded your destiny, how much control do you have over your future? How does free will influence your life? What is fate and what is destiny?

Decoding Our Reality

In *The Da Vinci Code*, Dan Brown presents us with a story that challenges our beliefs about religion, the Vatican, and church authority. The story is about hidden codes in

Da Vinci's paintings that reveal deeper mysteries, secret societies, Vatican conspiracies, and the identity of the Holy Grail. Coincidentally, this comes at a time when we are changing our beliefs about church authority and religion, when the papacy is in transition, and when the dark "secrets" of clerical behavior are being uncovered.

In *The Bible Code*, Michael Drosnin, with the help of a computer program, uncovers a code hidden in the Bible. He discovers that removing every fifth letter in the book creates a code that has predicted every major world event that has come to pass. A code of 5 also corresponds to the fifth dimension, the dimension beyond physical reality where thought manifests.

In *The God Code*, Greg Braden takes us a step further to show how God is coded into human DNA. He explains the relationship between the four levels of creation (creation, transformation, emanation, and density); the four elements that make up physical life (earth, fire, air, and water); and the four chemical elements of carbon, hydrogen, oxygen, and nitrogen; and he shows how they correspond to the four Hebrew letters that are the name of God, YHWH. By opening the door of our minds to the idea that our elemental cellular coding relates to God, it shows us that, in essence, we are God.

These books about decoding our reality are all appearing now because we are living in a time of evolution: We are being called to awaken and change the chaos of this time into order. If we can acknowledge that we are God, then we also acknowledge that it's our responsibility to participate in this change, and we will need some tools to help us.

Why Predictions Are Important

Change is the law of life.
And those who look into only to the past
or the present are certain to miss the future.

JOHN F. KENNEDY

I have been a professional metaphysical intuitive for twenty-five years. Every person who comes into my office has the same request: "Tell me what's going to happen in my future." Since the beginning of time, people have been looking to prophets for guidance, and they come to me for the same reason.

We humans have been learning about ourselves for thousands of years. We continue to grow in the process of understanding how we function, the amazing skills we possess, and the power that lies within us. We are so much more than we appear to be. Most of the time, though, we hold ourselves back, perhaps because we have abused our power in the past or are afraid to step beyond what we know. Whatever our reasons, the time for pretending we are unworthy has passed. Our mutual destiny is calling.

Every molecule of our being contains a wealth of intelligence, healing, and power, yet at this point in time, we still can't seem to decode the mysteries of life and death. Why are we born to die? What is death? Why are we so afraid to die?

Let's go back for a moment to the time of the Inquisition, when we were destroying those whose claims shook the foundations of society: Joan of Arc, for calling herself the messenger of God; Giordano Bruno, for telling us the Earth is round; or two thousand years ago, Jesus, for proclaiming himself the Son of God. Behind the desire to kill is fear. Fear still dominates our lives. It's because of our fear that we choose to be unsuccessful rather than successful.

We also have a tendency to be more negative than positive, which explains why so many people suffer from depression today. In fact, we depress the very feelings that connect us to our vitality and aliveness. When we look into our human past, we feel guilty for all the wrongdoings and blame them on our lack of evolution.

But at the level of consciousness, we have evolved a great deal. In recent years we have become more aware of our infinite possibilities and more open to the unknown, the paranormal, metaphysics, and the world beyond the physical dimension. Books about consciousness and personal transformation fill the bestseller lists. We watch television shows like *Medium* and movies like *The Sixth Sense* with great interest.

With motivation, willpower, and the desire to succeed, you can take responsibility for your life and alter your destiny. But how are you going to succeed if you don't know your skills and your potential, if you're in the wrong career, or if you don't trust your abilities and your intuitive mind? From the day we are born, we are told by our higher collective mind what to do. Most of the time, we don't listen.

Each of us was born with the ability to see into our future. Our mind is capable of breaking barriers of linear time and entering parts of the Invisible World and seeing many things. Yet we are often afraid of such power of seeing and knowing. So many people come to me and tell me they want to know their future but add, "Just tell me something good!" They don't want to face any pain, conflict, or misfortune that might lie ahead, confront karma to be resolved, or be questioned about their choices.

Predictions have a psychological effect on our mind. They help us open up to possibilities. But in and of themselves they don't create change or alter the law of cause and effect. When people are stuck, they come to me to get unstuck and to move their lives forward. Sometimes they are stuck in the belief that life is just happening to them and that I have the power to change things with my predictions—as if I have a magic wand.

As a metaphysical intuitive and psychologist, I can make you aware of the possibilities the future can hold. After all, when you know what's ahead, you can anticipate and plan for it. I also can give you specific information about your karma, past lives, and relationships as well as some details about the future. But for the most part, your future is up to you. I can help you project positive changes into your future and make better decisions, but only you can make it happen.

Only you are responsible for your own life, and yet over and over again I find that people don't want to acknowledge or accept their responsibility. But you have great power within yourself to control your destiny. In *Decoding Your Destiny*, I will help you see just how powerful you are, help you understand the difference between what is meant to be and what is free will, and provide tools that can help you predict and project your future.

What You Will Learn in This Book

Although people have been making predictions and prophecies since ancient times, there are many misconceptions about psychics and prophets, the powers they possess, and the science of prediction.

In part I of *Decoding Your Destiny*, "What Is Meant to Be," you will learn the difference between destiny and free will, prediction, and prophecy as well as how to work with the science of numerology to discover your soul code and life cycles.

The magic of creating your future begins with acknowledging that you have the ability to change by altering your thoughts and perceptions. Part II, "Opening Your Mind," explains how freeing yourself of skepticism, negativity, and resistance is the first step. Once the mind is open, I will show you how you can work with predictions to make the most of the information and insights you receive and how to ultimately predict and project your own future.

In part III, "Letting the Future In," you'll learn about brain function so you can make the most of its abilities, including specific guidance on becoming a master of your future and chapters devoted to "Tapping the Seven Tools of the Mind," "Developing Your Visionary Skills," and "Seven Steps to Master Your Future."

Projections: Three Steps to Programming the Mind

There are three steps to programming your mind so you can see and project your future.

First, as I explain in part II, you must acknowledge that you have the ability to predict your future, which means opening your mind and letting go of blocks and negativity. Believe in your heart that you can turn aspects of your life around.

Second, as I discuss in part III, know what it is you want and create a vision for it in your mind's eye. This means projecting a different life for yourself by broadening your level of perception.

Third, you must manifest your vision, acknowledging and using all the powers you possess within you, and then make a plan and stick to it. I have used this method in every aspect of my life with tremendous results, and I have also seen it work for my clients. You, too, can learn this process.

How We Can Change the World

If everyone projected positive energy into the world, not only would our individual lives change, but we could, through the collective consciousness, change the world itself. We could stop terrorism, a nuclear bomb explosion, or even war. These actions can all be prevented once we let go of the fear of our own power. Being afraid of our own power is choosing to live in fear and a state of paralysis. On one level, all the negative prophecies of the past have created negative thinking and negative actions, but we can turn all that around.

Our time has come. It is now within our power to change the outcomes of doom. We can reverse predictions and project a better, more peaceful reality if we all pull together. We can use all the ancient teachings and knowledge to prevent events from manifesting now. We truly can save the world.

Mankind has been obsessed with prophets' predictions that the world is about to end. Disasters prompted by comets and a shift of the Earth's poles have been predicted over and over again through thousands of years of evolution.

Both the mathematical interpretations of biblical prophecy and the writings in the Great Pyramid speak of a natural disaster or a cataclysm also known as the Rapture, which was to occur around 2000. The Rapture, defined as the transportation of the body and spirit, is predicted in the Bible in Thessalonians 4:15–17. According to the prophecies, this is the time when Christ will return and work against the Antichrist, bringing the worst and the best of times. The predictions apply to the years between 2000 and 2007.

It has also been said that the Antichrist will have the sign of the Beast (666) and that he will be a world leader worshipped by many. The Antichrist will work against the way of Christ, using fear to divide people instead of using love to unify.

All the prophecies talk about the years from 1992 to 2012 as the era of preparation for the New World. The Mayan calendar notes 2005 as a prophetic year. But all the predictions for the last thousands of years end in 2141. What is coming after that time has yet to be predicted.

In this time of great transformation, the problems we've created in the past are reflected back to us on both a personal and global scale. This moment in time is a turning point; the karma we have created is because we have not learned the lessons of our past and because we feel separated from the whole of creation. We have been pulled apart by beliefs based in limitation and fear, and we have moved away from what we truly are—the Divine.

But we have the power to choose differently because free will interferes with destiny. Free will is our most significant power: the power of becoming what we are meant to be. Free will and destiny work hand in hand. We can choose to look at prophecies differently and use them to help us reach the next stage of human evolution. By changing our point of view, we can see that some of the most important recent events are meant to help us learn and evolve as humans in this time of new beliefs.

The world is in a crisis, but we can choose to see this crisis as an opportunity to summon our courage and return to the primary source of life: Love.

PART I

Destiny: What Is Meant to Be

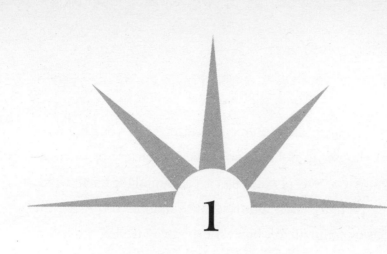

1

Your Soul Code:
The Road Map of Your Personality

Written within you is the code of life, or the code to your destiny—who you truly are and why you are here. Part of that code is written in the DNA of your body. But the other part, the agreement you made to be here on Earth, is coded in your soul and was written before you were born. The path your life takes depends on how you interact, in body and soul, with your destiny.

The moment of total transformation is the moment of birth. In that instant, you stepped through a door in time into a new reality—the reality of human life. The day of birth is the moment when the curtain goes up in your life. In that moment, you're a person with a character that's as unique as your DNA, ready to begin a play—the play of your life.

You have ultimate freedom to do with your life what you choose: to fulfill its potential completely or to create smaller versions of yourself, or your unfulfilled self, which only partially accomplishes your dharma. You make the decision to fulfill, to whatever extent you desire, the potential of life that exists within you.

The code of life gives you a broad outline of the opportunities, challenges, and lessons you will encounter in this life. Your code is the road you are traveling.

What Is Meant to Be

Certain aspects of your life are meant to be:

* The time and place of your birth

* Your physical appearance—your height and weight as well as any health problems you are predisposed to, as determined by your genetic code

* The people around you—those who come into your life are a reflection of your personal issues and often of karmic implications from past lives

* The skills, abilities, and energies you're born with

* The time of your death

All the rest is up to you. It's your decision to have children or not, to have money or not, to be successful or not. You are free to choose your relationships, your home, and your work in order to create what you want in your life. You are here to give birth to *you* in the limited time you are here. That is your free will, your willpower, and your responsibility. But without knowing what your destiny is, you can't make the most of your free will. Your life may be a series of stops and starts, missed opportunities, hardships, or repetitions of the same mistakes and lessons.

So how do we access this powerful information for ourselves? There are many powerful tools of divination and enlightenment available to us, but all divination begins with the knowledge passed down to us from the ancients, the knowledge upon which our understanding of our entire Universe is based. And that knowledge is numerology—the code of life.

Though this book is not intended to be a book about numerology, I want to explain this concept and its importance. Numerology is an ancient science relating numbers and harmonies in the creative process. Throughout ancient Mediterranean cultures, studying numerology was one of the paths to unity with God. For example, the mystical teachings of Judaism, called the *Kabala*, are based on a numerological interpretation of the Hebrew alphabet, in which each of the twenty-two letters can also be used as a number: aleph is 1; beth is 2, and so on. In the Jewish tradition, there are ten combinations of letters/numbers that are particularly harmonic, and these are called *sephirot*, or "enumerators." Together, they form the Tree of Life, which is a famous meditation diagram showing how all life comes into being. Four combinations of the *sephirot*, taken together, form a core harmonic pattern called the tetragrammaton, the unspeakable name of God (which is written in English as YHWH or JHVH). So, meditating on the numerological values of the Hebrew alphabet helps one to achieve union with the creative Source, which is God.

In the same way that the mystical study of alchemy led to chemistry and much of modern science, the study of numerology integrated with ancient Greek culture and led to geometry, axiomatic arithmetic, algebra, and higher mathematics—and so numerology is the basis for life in the modern world. Can you envision the world today without numbers? Without numerology, the world as we know it would not exist. We would not have mathematical chronology, the computer, or the electronic age. Numerology also gives us a valuable means to predict the future. In your own life, you can use it to understand your individual code and to master your destiny.

Numerology: The Code of Life

Spirit is vibration. Numbers are the expression of that vibration and the language of the Universe. As Pythagoras said, "Everything is according to numbers." Knowing your soul code offers you a map of your unique vibration to help you tap into your higher mind and discover why you are here and what you are meant to experience in life.

If you could interpret your genetic code, you'd have a wealth of information on what physical problems you are predisposed to and what you were born to experience. Our genes are passed down from our parents and grandparents; their messages and lessons are transferred to us, just as family karma is. But your numerological chart, like your astrological chart, is unique to you. What it reveals will help you project new possibilities into time to shape your future. A numerological interpretation of your birthday corresponds perfectly with your astrological reading. It offers you the same information but in a simple and more direct way.

The ancient Kabalists knew about the vibrations of numbers. They knew how numbers affect us physically, emotionally, and karmically. They recognized that the numbers 1 through 9 are each associated with a particular planet, and each number has its own energy that influences us—from how we behave to the state of our health. Most of us, however, don't immediately associate numbers with having particular vibrations or characteristics. We are not taught that the number 2 has a very different energy from the number 3.

Your Soul Code

Each of us has a soul code, a number that is based on our date of birth. This number indicates our temperament and personality traits as well as our physical vulnerabilities. Once you acknowledge your nature, you can use your free will to make the most of your gifts. You can also be honest about your weaknesses and consciously work on them. Knowing your soul code is like having a road map for your life. It can show you where you want to go and provide you with plenty of signposts on how to get there.

Your soul code is determined not only by the numbers in your date of birth but also by the numbers that are missing. We are all missing some numbers from our code because we are here on earth to achieve completion. In fact, the missing numbers could be the most revealing because they determine what challenges and lessons you will face in this life. By knowing your code, you will begin to understand the energies you're born with, the level of your soul's evolution—whether you are a young or old soul and what you are missing this time around—and the lessons you're here to learn.

How to Use Your Soul Code

When Erica came to me for a reading, I told her that her soul code revealed she was a 7, which meant that she had a lot of psychic abilities.

"It's like you have antenna," I told her, "and you are always receiving messages." Although she was in her fifties and had an established career in finance, Erica was open to the idea that she was psychic and that she had the potential to do spiritual work for a living. Encouraged by my revelation, Erica began developing her psychic abilities. Two years later, she called me to let me know that she had a successful business as a spiritual advisor and would soon be giving readings on the radio.

Like Erica, your soul code may reveal that you have a hidden ability to be financially successful in the material world or that you have a powerful need for independence. Knowing your natural gifts and inclinations, you can begin to develop your natural abilities, if you haven't already.

Calculating Your Soul Code

Calculating your soul code is easy to do.

1. Starting with your date of birth, add the numbers of the month you were born. January is 1, February is 2, and so on, through September, which is 9. October, the tenth month, becomes 1 (1 + 0 = 1), November is 2 (1 + 1 = 2), and December is 3 (1 + 2 = 3).

2. Then add the numbers of the day you were born. If your birthday is on the 23rd, you add 2 and 3 to get 5. If your birthday is on the 30th, you add 3 and 0 to get 3.

3. Then add the four digits of your birth year. If you were born in 1961, 1 + 9 + 6 + 1 = 17, and then you add the two digits 1 and 7 to get 8. Here's another example: 1975 is 1 + 9 + 7 + 5 = 22; 2 + 2 = 4.

4. Next, add your three numbers together, and reduce the two-digit number by adding the individual digits together to get a one-digit number, which is also called a "pure number."

Let's say Lisa was born 1-3-1970. If we add all the numbers together, reducing them to digits, we get 3: 1 + 3 + 1 + 9 + 7 + 0 = 21; 2 + 1 = 3. So Lisa's primary soul code is 3. There are also other significant numbers and calculations to look at. In Lisa's case, the energy of her soul code is even stronger because her actual date of birth is a 3 as well.

Calculating Lisa's Soul Code: The Reverse Pyramid

January 3, 1970
Month = 1
Day = 3
Year = 1+ 9 + 7 + 0 = 17

---

1 + 3 plus 1 + 7 = 4 + 8
4 + 8 = 12
1 + 2 = 3
3

The numbers 11, 22, 33, and 44 do not get reduced to a 2, 4, 6, or 8. These are master numbers which reveal that you are a person on a mission who is destined to live an extraordinary life. Al Gore is such a person. While he may not have become president, he is destined to do great things because his primary soul code is 11: his birthday is March 31, 1948 (again, if we add all the numbers together, 3 + 3 + 1 + 1 + 9 + 4 + 8 = 29; 2 + 9 = 11). Other 11s include Buddha (4/8/529 B.C.), Jesus (traditionally 12/25/1 A.D.), Bill Clinton (8/19/1946), and Tony Blair (5/6/1953).

Because we are working with just nine numbers, many people ask me, "What happens when people share the same numbers? Are their lives the same?" Sharing the same numbers with someone shows that you have a lot in common and that you will face many similar lessons. What differentiates us, however, is our willpower and how we make use of our talents and our perceptions—in other words, how we choose to look at life.

Numbers and Their Planets

The attributes of each number are based on a corresponding planet. By the word *planet*, I use the ancient Greeks' interpretation, which considered planets, including the Sun and the Moon, as heavenly objects. In astrology, each planet exerts its influence on us. Based on the movement of each planet through our solar system, during some months one planet may have a stronger influence on us than others. Likewise, if the planet that corresponds with the main number in your soul code is weak during a certain month, that's a month when the Universe is not very supportive of you in any of your efforts. For example, if you are a 1, your energy is that of the Sun; this means March, April, July, and August are far better months for supporting you than October, November, and December, when the Sun's influence is weaker.

A Numerological Key

1. The Sun

Main attributes. 1 is ruled by the Sun, which rules our solar system. The Sun holds the energy of leadership and intellect.

Because 1s have the Sun's energy, they not only have lots of ideas, but they also have the self-discipline to carry them out. Ambitious and fearless, they are natural-born leaders. They are often very serious and love to teach and be taught. 1s are hardworking, smart, organized, neat, and productive. 1s are pioneers and are adventurous and driven by their own convictions.

When it comes to relationships, 1s know how to make others happy, are highly attentive, love children, and have great social abilities. They often have to deal with a domineering parent during childhood, and they marry early in life. They are energetic and healthy. But they have a tendency to work too much, and their health may suffer as a result.

Favorable periods for 1s are months when the Sun is strong (March, April, July, and August). Less favorable times are when the Sun is weak (October, November, and December).

According to the teachings of the Kabala, the Sun is associated with the head and rules the right side of the body, the left hemisphere of the brain, and the right eye. Physically, 1s are most vulnerable in these areas and are prone to headaches, bone problems, and arthritis.

Attributes 1s need to work on. 1s have difficulty expressing love and can be stubborn, overly cautious about money, jealous, and overcritical.

Famous 1s. Larry King (11/28/1933) and Dick Cheney (1/30/1941)

Missing 1s. People who are missing 1 from their soul code must learn the lessons of independence, courage, identity, finding oneself, hard work, creative thinking, and problem solving.

2. The Moon

Main attributes. 2 is ruled by the Moon, which reflects light from the Sun and holds the maternal energy of cooperation, balance, partnership, and understanding. 2s tend to be good listeners and are diplomatic and tactful. They are often quiet, shy, and humble, as well as intelligent and temperamental. 2s work on realizing dreams, love making friends, and greatly enjoy entertainment and leisure. They tend to be romantic, but because they are not naturally demonstrative, they don't often show it. 2s are frequently born into a family where there is a lot of criticism, and as a result, they often grow up with low self-confidence.

Strong periods for 2s are June and July. Weak periods are December, January, and February.

The Moon rules over the left eye, the left side of the body, and the right hemisphere of the brain, as well as the neck, which makes 2s prone to sore throats, tonsillitis, and thyroid problems. The Moon is associated with emotions, so 2s are also prone to nervous conditions and indigestion.

Attributes 2s need to work on. 2s are superstitious and often rebellious when restricted. They are emotional and often insecure. Because they often try to repress their feelings, when they do express themselves, it can come out as flashes of anger or oversensitivity.

Famous 2s. Madonna (8/17/1958), Henry Kissinger (5/17/1923), Karen Carpenter (3/2/1950), and Edgar Allan Poe (1/19/1809).

Missing 2s. People who are missing 2 from their soul code must learn the lessons of creating and maintaining good relationships and partnerships: trust, building security, setting boundaries, learning to communicate, and giving support to others. The challenge for 2s is to feel safe emotionally in order to be available for relationships. Women who are missing 2 also have to learn the lesson of the mother: they may have difficulty becoming a mother or relating to their mother or their daughter. Men who are missing 2 lack female energy. This could mean they will have trouble finding a wife, lose or have a distant relationship with their mother, or experience some other loss of a mother, wife, or daughter.

3. Jupiter

Main attributes. 3 has the energy of Jupiter, the planet of courage, power, hard work, energy, and knowledge. It is considered the lucky planet and has a powerful form of energy. 3 is the code of creativity, beauty, and the good life. 3s are emotional, self-expressive, and gifted with eloquence and musical talent. They have lovely voices and often have careers in the arts, media, or education. They are often fascinating, well informed, altruistic, and creative. They are naturally honest, trustworthy, appreciative, and observant. They also love attention and decorating the home.

Favorable periods for 3s are February, March, and December. Less favorable periods are October and November.

Jupiter rules the liver and the area between the waist and the thighs. 3s are therefore prone to liver, kidney, and skin problems and emotional disturbances.

Attributes 3s need to work on. 3s have trouble with moodiness, impulsiveness, hasty decision making, vengefulness, and secretiveness; and they are easily angered.

Famous 3s. Judy Garland (7/10/1922), Jennifer Lopez (7/24/1970), and Hillary Rodham Clinton (10/26/1947).

Missing 3s. People who are missing 3 from their soul code need to learn the lesson of discovering self-expression, creativity, and the artistic self. This is the lesson of being in touch with your inner world and your dreams, appreciating the imagination, and balancing life's demands with beauty and creativity.

4. Uranus

Main attributes. 4 is the energy of Uranus, the planet of discipline, grounding, and structure. 4s are active, dynamic, diplomatic, self-motivated, determined, loving, caring, brave, and generous. They tend to have a good memory. 4s are generally hardworking and loyal and have a strong sense of dignity. They usually achieve wealth and power, often through inheritance or real estate, and they are interested in inventing new ways of doing things.

The strong periods for 4s are March, April, July, and August. Weak periods are October, November, and December.

Uranus rules the heart, and 4s may suffer from sickness in the head or chest, bone disorders, and backaches.

Attributes 4s need to work on. 4s are overly emotional, quick to anger, frustrated, rigid, aggressive, stubborn, and unimaginative.

Famous 4s. Donald Trump (6/14/1946), Bill Gates (10/28/1955), John Kerry (12/11/1943), and Oprah Winfrey (1/29/1954).

Missing 4s. People who are missing 4 from their soul code must learn the lessons of achievement through planning, hard work, and discipline.

5. Mercury

Main attributes. 5 is ruled by the planet Mercury. It is the energy of the intellect, independence, and freedom. 5s are strong-willed and driven, and they love their freedom. They are intelligent and have deep feelings, good physical energy, and strong intuition. Fives are understanding, progressive, and adaptable. They are elevated thinkers who like to think outside the box. They love literature, the arts, and things of beauty. Fives also love to dream, and they are wanderers who enjoy traveling. 5s have difficulties being attached to people for a significant amount of time. In love, they want a lot of freedom and independence. They tend to marry later in life and have fewer children because they have trouble being tied down.

Favorable periods for 5s are May, June, August, and most of September. Weak periods are the end of September and December.

Mercury is the planet associated with the lungs. 5s may have lung problems or difficulty with breathing. They tend to suffer from sickness in the ear and neck or have liver problems as well as constipation. 5s can be fragile, but they usually live long lives.

Attributes 5s need to work on. 5s have a tendency to be stubborn and spendthrift and have difficulties with intimacy.

Famous 5s. Benjamin Franklin (1/17/1706—a double 5, with a 5 both as his soul code and year of birth), Thomas Jefferson (4/13/1773), Johnny Carson (10/23/1925—also a double 5 because of his soul code and day of birth), and Helen Keller (6/27/1880).

Missing 5s. People who are missing 5 from their soul code must learn the lessons of adapting to sudden changes, generosity, maintaining good health, and freedom. Because 5 is the male energy, women who are missing 5 often have difficulty finding a husband or are missing the male energy in some other way, such as not having a father present in their lives when they are younger. A woman may be able to find this male energy by having a son even if she does not marry. If a man is missing 5, he has to learn the lesson of both becoming a father and being a son.

6. Venus

Main attributes. 6 is the energy of Venus, the planet of service, responsibility, emotional harmony, and nurturing. 6s are kind, polite, soft-spoken, funny, temperamental, friendly, humorous, and talkative. They have lots of ideas, an active mind, and a passion for life. 6s are concerned for others, and they possess a strong need to serve and help.

Strong periods for 6s are April, September, and most of October. Weak periods are the end of October, November, and January.

Venus rules the stomach and genital area, so 6s are most vulnerable to stomach and urinary problems, gall bladder problems, and venereal diseases, as well as congestion.

Attributes 6s need to work on. 6s sometimes suffer from negative thoughts, anxiety, dark moods, and angry outbursts; and they are easily bored, fussy, narrow-minded, easily hurt, and take a long time to heal.

Famous 6s. Eleanor Roosevelt (10/11/1884), Albert Einstein (3/14/1870), and Christopher Reeve (9/25/1952).

Missing 6s. People who are missing 6 from their soul code need to learn the lessons of family, home, community, loving and being loved, service to society and the world, and teaching.

7. Neptune

Main attributes. 7 is the energy of the planet Neptune, the planet of wisdom, spirituality, intuition, and self-knowledge.

7s are logical and honest. They are deep thinkers and are involved in the mysteries of life and death. They are fun to be with, quiet, friendly, approachable, caring, forgiving, and sympathetic. 7s love to be alone.

The strongest periods for 7s are June and July. Less favorable periods are January and February.

Neptune rules the glands and blood. 7s may have stomach and dietary problems as well as weakness in the pancreas and spleen, glandular problems, infections, and gout.

Attributes 7s need to work on. 7s are secretive, moody, unassertive, and easily hurt.

Famous 7s. Stephen Hawking (1/8/1942), Princess Diana (7/1/1961), and Muhammad Ali (1/17/1942).

Missing 7s. People who are missing 7 from their soul code must learn the lessons of intellectual and spiritual seeking and contemplating the mysteries of life.

8. Saturn

Main attributes. 8 is the energy of Saturn, the planet of karma. 8s are goal-oriented, driven, and motivated and are able to manifest success in the material world. They enjoy having power and being in authority because they are natural-born leaders, and they are good at supervising and managing others and at making money. 8s are attractive, caring, suave, brave, firm, independent, and romantic. They love to dream and are talented in arts and music.

Strong periods for 8s are September, October, January, and February. Weak periods are December, March, and April.

Saturn is the ruler of the legs, so 8s are prone to rheumatism and paralysis, as well as deafness and asthma. They are prone to illnesses such as indigestion, high blood pressure, and ulcers.

Attributes 8s need to work on. 8s are quick to anger, jealousy, and have difficulty relaxing.

Famous 8s. Barbara Bush (11/4/1946), Nancy Reagan (6/7/1921), Paul Newman (1/26/1925), and James Carville (10/25/1944).

Missing 8s. People who are missing 8 from their soul code must learn the lessons of negotiation, handling power, supervision, authority, achieving success, investing, and making money.

9. Mars and Pluto

Main attributes. 9 is the energy of Mars and Pluto. It's the energy of idealism, humanitarianism, altruism, extreme generosity, and sacrifice. 9s have a divine purpose and embrace the spiritual path. Because they have the energy of Pluto, the planet of destruction, 9s experience a lot of sorrow, illness, and loss, which gives them a greater understanding of life's purpose. 9s are cool, calm, clever, confident, and optimistic. They love sports, have a good memory, and are loyal, honest, and talkative.

For 9s, strong periods are mid-March to mid-April, late October, and November. Weak periods are early March, May, June, and the beginning of October.

Mars rules the muscular system and the bone marrow, and Pluto is the ruler of the immune system. 9s may have respiratory, digestive, and emotional problems, as well as infections and problems with their bones and muscles.

Attributes 9s need to work on. 9s can be overly critical, compulsive, and secretive; and they bottle up their feelings.

Famous 9s. Jimmy Carter (10/1/1924), Gandhi (10/2/1869), and George Harrison (2/25/1944).

Missing 9s. People who are missing 9 from their soul code need to learn the lessons of universal brotherhood, compassion, high ideals, humanitarianism, and working for the greater good for bringing hope and peace.

11. The Master Number

Main attributes. 11 is a master number. 11s desire to serve humanity to bring peace and reconciliation. They are visionaries and leaders. Famous politicians and religious leaders are often 11s. They have the same characteristics, physical vulnerabilities, and strong and weak periods that 2s have, but they can also see the larger picture and take into account the needs of many people.

Famous 11s. Al Gore (3/31/1948), Bill Clinton (8/19/1946), Ronald Reagan (2/6/1911), Martin Luther King Jr. (1/15/1948), Tony Blair (5/6/1953), Buddha (4/8/529 B.C.), and Jesus (traditionally 12/25/1 A.D.).

How to Interpret Your Soul Code

Lisa has a primary number of 3 in her soul code. This number corresponds to Jupiter, the planet of courage, power, hard work, energy, and knowledge. It is a lucky planet with a powerful form of energy. Lisa, like others who have a 3 as their primary soul code, is active, ambitious, and disciplined, and she believes strongly in education.

In Lisa's date of birth she has two 1s, 3, 7, and 9. If we add up the numbers in her year of birth, we get 8. But adding up the month of her birth, the day, the year—separately or all together—does not yield any 2s, 4s, 5s, or 6s.

Because the Moon represents the mother lesson, missing the 2 in her code means that Lisa is destined to learn significant lessons from her relationship with her mother as well as from being a mother herself. One of her life challenges is to identify and resolve the karma with her mother and her daughter. In fact, Lisa's mother was very domineering, which affected Lisa's relationships with men. In her relationship with her daughter, however, Lisa is determined to be the kind of mother that she wished she'd had.

In missing 4, the planet Uranus, Lisa must work hard on learning the lessons of material order, grounding, and financial stability. She also needs to project a better image of herself at work and attract more money.

Without 5, the planet Mercury, Lisa is missing the male energy of freedom and independence. Throughout her life she was estranged from her father and had difficulty freeing herself from the influence of a controlling mother.

Missing 6, the influence of Venus, brings the challenge of learning the lessons of commitment and love. In Lisa's case, she did not have children, nor did she find a husband until late in life. Her major lesson in this life is to find happiness in her marriage and remain committed to her family.

The Other Numbers in Your Soul Code

Just as in astrology, where the characteristics of your Sun sign might sometimes be overshadowed by the characteristics of a rising planet in your chart, in numerology you are influenced by numbers in your soul code besides your primary number. For example, if you have an 11 in your code, you will hold a higher vibration and have the potential to be a visionary leader.

The primary number of your soul code can also be overshadowed by your day of birth, the year, and the month, usually in that order. In most cases, the code of the day you were born is more likely to influence you than the code of the month.

Repeating Numbers

If a number appears more than once in your soul code, it will have a stronger influence on you. Peter, born 9/8/1953, has a primary soul code of 8, plus an 8 in his birth date, as well as two 9s in his birth date. A very powerful spiritual number, 9 shows that he is an old soul. The two 9s dominate the influence of the 8s. Peter was actually surprised to learn that he is an 8 because the 9 energy was so dominant in his life. Learning that he is an 8 helped him to rethink what his natural talents are. Because he has only 8s and 9s in his code and is missing so many of the other numbers, he clearly has many lessons to learn in this lifetime.

Benjamin Franklin was a double 5, with a 5 both as his primary soul code and year of birth. Besides helping to create the Declaration of Independence and being thrilled by intellectual pursuits, Franklin was a man who loved his personal freedom and enjoyed traveling. Thomas Jefferson, who was also a 5, was a traveler as well. Clearly he was a lover of intellectual pursuits and a man who cherished independence.

Relationships and Your Soul's Compatibility

It's important that your soul code complements that of the people in your life. If you discover you are not compatible with a primary person in your life, you will have to do a lot of work to get along, whether it is a relationship in love, in business, or with a family member or friend.

Kelly had a long business relationship with her friend Sandra, but they were always at odds with each other. They had very different ideas about how to present themselves as a team and how to run the business. On top of this, the more time they spent with each other, the more they were bothered by each other's differences. Ultimately, they had to end both their business partnership and their friendship.

Kelly felt bad about how things had ended and was reluctant to believe that they couldn't patch up the relationship. I explained to Kelly that her soul code was a 5, while her friend's was a 9, which made them very incompatible. As a 5, Kelly needed freedom and independence, while as a 9, Sandra had a higher level of spirituality and wisdom and was more grounded, more giving, and more attached. Knowing this, Kelly was able to accept that intensifying her relationship with her friend had been a mistake and that their fundamental incompatibility had been too strong for their friendship to survive.

Long-married political couples often have complementary codes. Ronald Reagan was born 2/6/1911, making him an 11. The planets Venus and Jupiter are in the year of his life, and these, along with the Moon, are his major energies. He is missing Neptune, Uranus, and Saturn. Nancy Reagan was born 6/7/1921, making her an 8, which is Saturn. 6 is Venus, 7 is Neptune, and 1921 is a 4, which is Uranus, so she has the exact planets her husband was missing. 8s and 11s are opposite forms of energy: 8s deal with the material, and 11s deal with the spiritual. Both Ronald and Nancy Reagan needed each other to complete the cycle of their lives. Also, both have a 6 in their birthdays, which is a karmic connection.

Compatibility between Numbers

* 1 is especially good with the independent 5 and also good with 1, 2, and 3. 1 works with 7 and 9 only in special circumstances.

✳ 2 is good with 1, 4, 6, and 8.

✳ 3 is good with 1, 3, 5, 6, and 9.

✳ 4 is good with 1, 2, 6, and 7, and sometimes 3 and 8.

✳ 5 is good with 1 and 9, and sometimes 3, 6, and 7.

✳ 6 is good with 2, 3, 4, 8, and 9.

✳ 7 is good with 3, 4, and 5, and sometimes 7.

✳ 8 is good with 1, 2, 3, 4, and 6.

✳ 9 is good with 3, 5, 6, 7, and 9, and sometimes 4.

The Pinnacles

The Pinnacles are the four stages or cycles of changes in your life that are preordained at birth. Knowing them can reveal what lies ahead of us on our life's journey. The first and fourth pinnacles last thirty years, and the second and the third pinnacles last nine years.

Pinnacle 1. The first pinnacle is about development and soul searching. During this time you will explore questions about your personal existence, your inner world, and your spiritual growth. The first pinnacle is from birth to approximately age thirty, depending on your soul code.

Pinnacle 2. The second pinnacle is approximately between the ages of thirty and forty. This is when you identify your larger purpose in life and begin to feel a need to find your social responsibility.

Pinnacle 3. The third pinnacle is between ages forty and forty-nine. This is the time for increasing your personal power and your financial success.

Pinnacle 4. The fourth pinnacle is from age forty-nine through the next thirty years. During this time you learn to maintain balance between heaven and earth.

The transition from one pinnacle to the next is strongly felt, especially between the first and second. This is a transition from one stage of evolution to another. The first stage of evolution is when you discover yourself. The second stage is when you put yourself in motion to achieve what you're here for. It's a big shift from being in your own world to projecting yourself in the world. As this shift occurs, you feel more responsible for what you are creating in the world.

How to Calculate the Four Pinnacles

Pinnacle 1. To calculate the number of your first pinnacle, add the month of your birth to the day and reduce it to a single number. For example, for March 25, the first pinnacle is 1 (3 + 2 + 5 = 10; 1 + 0 = 1).

Pinnacle 2. To calculate the second pinnacle, add together the birth date and year and reduce it to a single digit. So for March 25, 1955, the second pinnacle is 9 (2 + 5 + 1 + 9 + 5 + 5 = 27; 2 + 7 = 9).

Pinnacle 3. To calculate the third pinnacle, add the first pinnacle to the second pinnacle. For the example above, the third pinnacle is 1 (1 + 9 = 10; 1 + 0 =1).

Pinnacle 4. To calculate the fourth pinnacle, add the birth month and the year and reduce it to a single digit. For March 1955, the fourth pinnacle is 5 (3 + 1 + 9 + 5 + 5 = 23; 2 + 3 = 5).

Example: George W. Bush (7/6/1946)

Pinnacle 1. 4 (7 + 6 = 13; 1 + 3 = 4)

Pinnacle 2. 8 (6 + 1 + 9 + 4 + 6 = 26; 2 + 6 = 8)

Pinnacle 3. 3 (4 + 8 = 12; 1 + 2 = 3)

Pinnacle 4. 9 (7 + 1 + 9 + 4 + 6 = 27; 2 + 7 = 9)

The Meaning of the Pinnacle Numbers

Once you have a number for each pinnacle, use the following guide to determine what that number indicates for your pinnacle.

* 1 is the time when you try to attain independence

* 2 is the time of union, partnership, and cooperation

* 3 is the time of emotion, creativity, and making money

* 4 is the time to build a home; a period of discipline and responsibility

* 5 is the time of change, adaptation, and freedom

* 6 is the time for love, marriage, family, and children; the time of balance

* 7 is the time for study, research, and understanding the principles of living

* 8 is the time to manage prosperity, career, and success

* 9 is the time to learn tolerance and compassion; the time to uplift others; the time of maturity

As you go through your life, it is important to recognize the themes of life you're experiencing. For example, is it a time in your life when you're trying to attain independence? Or is it a time for love, marriage, and family? Is it a time to concentrate on tolerance and compassion? Or is it a time to focus on being creative and making money? When you become aware of what theme your pinnacle indicates, you can focus your perception exactly on what is meant for you to achieve in that period of time. For example, if it is a period of discipline and responsibility and building a home, which is pinnacle four, you can concentrate on developing the abilities and the skills needed for that particular task.

2

Your Personal Years and the Cycles of Seven

The Personal Year

An important aspect of working with the soul code is determining your code for any given year. Calculating what year you are in can help you determine which years are better than others for starting projects or major life events, such as a marriage, a business, or a career. Once you become familiar with your cycle of personal years, you can make the most of the times when the Universe is working with you and avoid fighting the times when it isn't. Because personal years run in cycles of nine, you can start with the year you are currently in and project your future to plan certain events in accordance with their optimal times.

Personal years are excellent to keep in mind when you're maintaining a calendar or daily planner.

To calculate your personal year, add the number of your birth month plus your birth date to the year you want to look at. Going back to Lisa, born January 3, the year 2005 would be her personal year 2 $(1 + 3 + 2 + 0 + 0 + 5 = 11; 1 + 1 = 2)$, which is a year of delays and disappointments.

Key to Personal Years 1 through 9

Personal Year 1. This is a year of tremendous importance because in personal year 1 you control your destiny more so than at any other time of your life. In this year, you are setting a course that will determine whether you will be happy or unhappy, successful or unsuccessful, over the next nine years. Whatever you plan this year will have longevity. It is a time during which you will find it easier to summon your inner strength and courage. Most importantly, this is the year to plant the seeds for the projects that are most important to you, as they have the best chance of blossoming and bearing fruit. If you plant nothing now and wait until a later year, you will not yield the best possible crop. This is the best year to marry, begin a business, and start making major life changes, such as buying a home or making a major geographical move.

Personal Year 2. The second personal year is a time of delays and disappointments. In this year the forces in the Universe block your energy, thwarting even the most well-constructed plans. The key to making it through this year is patience and acceptance. You will probably lose something important to you during year 2. It might be a romance that goes sour or an opportunity that slips out of your hands. Personal year 2 is also an excellent year for reconciliation in relationships. If you have been unable to make peace with someone, try to do so in this year. This is a period of germination and gestation, a slow-moving year that is favorable for planting seeds of love and new romance. Getting married is a good idea in your personal year 2, although personal year 1 is the best time.

Personal Year 3. This is a year of opportunities and pleasures. The accent is on beauty, harmony, and forgiveness. If you would like to end a relationship, this is the best time to do so. If you marry during this time, you will be going against the energy of this year. Personal year 3 is generally a good year for generating income and saving money, but not good for investments. For example, you might add to a bank account you already have because you have extra money, but this would not be a good time to invest that extra money in a business. It would be wiser to sell items you no longer need and accumulate material wealth rather than begin any financial ventures. This is also a good year for meeting people. Those you welcome into your life this year will help and enrich you. If possible, however, avoid entering into any major commitments or intense friendships in this year. Projects started in personal year three are fated to be short-lived. If you marry, begin a business, or start a major undertaking, such as quitting smoking or dieting and exercising, you'll find yourself in a difficult struggle.

Personal Year 4. This is the year to nurture the plans you made in personal year 1 and to watch your projects grow. It is an excellent year to establish a relationship and to work out family problems. New friendships made in personal year 4 will enrich you and be long-lasting. However, endings to relationships will be problematic this year. If you divorce your spouse or leave your church or social group, the situation may be especially rancorous. But while beginnings involving family and relationships will work out well this year, other big changes will not. The Universe will not support speculative investments or job or career changes. Because 4 and 8 are numbers of karma, personal year 4 is a year of facing the consequences of actions from your past. Personal year 4 is a time to step back and look at your life. Use this year to improve your home and your health, but without undertaking major changes, such as buying a house or quitting smoking. Instead, work on self-discipline and getting more organized.

Personal Year 5. This is the year of change, a time that brings freedom from problems as well as opportunities to improve your life. Personal year 5 is a vacation period, a perfect time to travel and focus your mind on higher matters and ideals instead of being caught up in everyday life. This is not the time to start a new business. Year 5 has a vibration of love and pregnancy. It is easiest to get pregnant in year 5. Your finances may fluctuate in this year, but overall they will be good. You can use the energy of this year to your advantage by keeping your mind open to new ways of doing things and expanding projects you already have underway. This year is also good for advertising, promotion, and enlarging what already exists in your life.

Personal Year 6. This is the most pleasant of all years. It is a period of success. This is a year free of financial problems and a time to make adjustments to your work and come up with new ideas. You can also let go of projects that are not working for you. Personal year 6 brings divine protection. It has a domestic and positive vibration. This is a good year for strengthening your relationship with your spouse and children and for taking care of your home. The energy of 6 supports your commitment to your family. This is also a good year for healing wounds and making peace with your enemies. The vibration of personal year 6 is good for the arts as well as for serving others. It is a blossoming time.

Personal Year 7. God created the world in six days, and on the seventh day, God rested. Personal year 7 is a time for you to rest and to plan for what you want to manifest in personal year 8. This is a year of patience and waiting. Do not invest or plant the seeds for your future. Instead, meditate, travel, be introspective, and examine the mistakes of the past. This is a year for solitude, peace, and wisdom. Do not force any issues or lose control. Avoid making any major moves this year; stay in your home and at your current job, if possible.

Personal Year 8. This is the year of karma, and the karmic impact can be twice as hard as in personal year 4, especially in dealing with the fallout of past actions. Personal year 8 is a year of achievements and accomplishments, a time when you see the material rewards of your efforts.

Money will come from unexpected sources, and you will be presented with many opportunities, recognitions, and honors. It is an excellent time to look for a new job or start a new career. This is a year for material manifestation, so ventures begun this year can work out well, especially if you begin them in the first six months of the year.

Personal Year 9. Personal year 9 is a time to finish projects you have begun and a time to collect your karma if you did not do so in personal year 8. It is a year in which to let go of things, not to begin them. This is not a year to marry, and if you separate from your spouse this year, reconciliation will be extremely difficult. This is also the year to drop relationships and projects that have drained you. It's a good time to study, write, and plan events for the next year. It is a time for getting your affairs in order and cleaning up after the harvest of personal year 8.

The Personal Month

Within your personal year are personal months. To determine your personal month, add the number of your day of birth to the month you want to look at.

If your day of birth is 25 and you want to look at March, add 2 + 5 to get 7 and then 7 + 3 to get 10 = 1. Just like personal years, personal months fall in cycles of nine. So if March is 1, you can lay out the other months to plan and foresee your entire year: January = 8, February = 9, March = 1, April = 2, and so on.

Here are some of the indications for the personal months 1 through 9.

Personal Month 1. This month brings a sense of freshness and a new beginning in your personal life and career. You are more energetic and decisive. This is a time of opportunity and a time when you need to adapt quickly to a new endeavor to move your career forward. Financially it is not the best time. If you're single, you will be introduced to someone. The attraction is likely to be immediate, but relationships under this number tend to burn quickly.

Personal Month 2. In the second personal month you will have greater insight into other people's emotions. You might feel some instability, so this is not a good time to take financial risks. It is the time, however, to release some bottled-up feelings. Romance is also important this month, as you'll have a desire to seek deeper meaning and values. Communication is key. Travel is also beneficial during this period.

Personal Month 3. Money matters come to the foreground in personal month 3. Debts owed to you will be paid. Your ability to promote yourself is great. A career change is possible. This is a month in which you'll be more creative. It's also a great time to reach out to relatives and old friends or to take a vacation.

Personal Month 4. This is the month to commit, to be responsible, and to act rather than procrastinate. Personal month 4 can bring success, but it depends on your willingness to stand up for yourself and take appropriate action. This is a good time to make fundamental long-term changes in your life. It is also important to demonstrate to others that you are dependable.

Personal Month 5. The fifth personal month is the time to let go of old plans, concepts, and projects that aren't working or don't bring fulfillment. This is an adventurous, dynamic, and progressive time when you should spend less time focusing on details and routine activities. Attending social events is important. Any relationships started now will have emotional depth and will teach you about love and life. Be open to all possibilities this month, but take care of your health.

Personal Month 6. This month brings stability to the changes in personal month 5. Expect recognition, a raise, or a promotion. This is the month to shift the focus to your relationship with your family. Loyalty and trust are fundamental to your well-being this month. If you're single, you will find someone for a long-lasting relationship. Health problems will take a turn for the better.

Personal Month 7. This month, focus on your inner self. You will be inspired to refine your understanding of your place in the Universe. Search your soul, define your priorities, and plan the future. Put romance, career, and financial matters on the back burner this month. There will be time to deal with them later. If you use this time to focus on honest self-confrontation, it will ensure your progress.

Personal Month 8. This month will reward you in many ways. This is the time for money and business. It is an excellent time to promote your ideas. Expect recognition. This month is favorable for romance and expressing your love.

Personal Month 9. The ninth personal month brings a lot of completion in your life. It is the time to let go and prepare for new adventures. You are moving into the spotlight, so self-promotion is favorable. Discipline is also needed. Some people may be leaving, while new people are coming into your life. While you'll feel emotional and vulnerable during this time, you'll also be ready to change.

Planning Events Using Your Personal Years and Months

At the beginning of the karmic cycle of nine years, the Universe supports you as you plant seeds throughout the cycle. If you begin a project in personal year 1, you have the best chance for success. If you must start a new project and year 1 has already passed, try to start it in year 8. Years 3 and 6 are also good years for beginnings, but they are not as powerful as 1 or 8. When the nine-year cycle is complete and you enter a new personal year 1, you must recommit yourself to the project you started or begin a new one.

In my own life, I have worked with personal years very consciously. I was a singer for nine years and again in a second cycle of nine. But when the next cycle of nine came around, I decided to move on to something new and focused on working with my psychic gifts. Nine years later, I began to think about writing books. Nine years after that, I started my jewelry business. I have been successful in each of these endeavors, partly because I worked with the energetic cycles of personal years, maximizing my chances for success.

Because all dates have codes, you can plan an important event to occur on a day of a particular energy to give it the best chance of flourishing. For instance, my friend Kathy married her husband, Peter, on May 25, 1996. This date was a personal year 1 for the marriage itself, so it was a perfect day for a wedding because the Universe supported the beginning of a marriage on this date. However, on May 25, 2005, Kathy and Peter's marriage will enter a personal year 1 again, so they must make an extra effort to examine their relationship and commit themselves to deepening their intimacy, trust, and passion. If they do this and work with the Universe's flow of energy, they stand the best possible chance of keeping their marriage strong.

You can also plan an event to make use of the energy of a different number. Because 9 is an energy for tying up loose ends and saying good-bye forever, you might plan to quit a job or break off a problematic relationship on a date with the energy of 9. In doing so, you are supported by the energetic flow of the Universe, which will minimize any pain or difficulty associated with the ending.

Recent U.S. Presidents' Personal Years

It's interesting to calculate the personal years for recent U.S. presidents. President Clinton was born on 8/19/1946, so in 1998, he was in a personal year 9, a time when the Universe supports endings. It is also a year when we face any karma we did not resolve. Clinton's interactions with Monica Lewinsky, which occurred in 1997, his personal year 8, became publicly known in January 1998. Impeachment proceedings against him began in November 1998, but he was not successfully impeached because the process dragged out so long that he was able to resolve his karma. At the same time, he was on the verge of a powerful personal year 1. Had impeachment taken place earlier, or had Clinton avoided dealing with his karma, he might have been ousted from office.

Personal years also affect elections. In the election of 2000, Al Gore, born 3/31/1948, was in a personal year 9, a time of endings ($3 + 3 + 1 + 2 + 0 + 0 + 0 = 9$), while George W. Bush, born 7/6/1946, was in a personal year 6 ($7 + 6 + 2 + 0 + 0 + 0 = 15; 1 + 5 = 6$), a time of flourishing and success.

Four years later, in the election of November 2004, George W. Bush was in a personal year 1 ($7 + 6 + 2 + 0 + 0 + 4 = 19; 1 + 9 = 10; 1 + 0 = 1$), which is the most powerful personal year, the year of great opportunities. Even though he faced some challenges astrologically, he was able to win the election and make a new beginning. His opponent, John Kerry, born 12/11/1943, was in a personal year 2 (1 + 2 + 1 + 1 + 2 + 0 + 0 + 4 =11; 1 + 1 = 2). The universal energy favored Bush.

Although the candidates have not been named, looking ahead to the presidential election of 2008, Hillary Rodham Clinton, born 10/26/1947, will be just starting a personal year 1 when the election is held. Rudolph Giuliani, born 5/28/1944, will be in a personal year 7, which is not a good year for a presidential run, and John McCain, born 8/29/1936, will be in a personal year 2, which is probably the worst year in which to try to attain a big goal.

Points of Destiny

When the energy of a personal year matches the path of your life, it is indeed a point of destiny. One example is the date the U.S. Declaration of Independence was adopted, 7/4/1776. The date itself is a 5, and the document was written by Thomas Jefferson, who is a 5, and edited by Benjamin Franklin, who is a double 5. This is a powerful example of a point in destiny for these two men who were destined to achieve the freedom they sought.

The Seven-Year Cycle:

Where You Are Now

In addition to knowing who we are and what our lessons in life will be, we all need to know what cycle of our lives we are in. It is important to know which planet's influence you are under at any particular time in your life. For example, under the influence of Mercury, the ages of twenty-one to twenty-eight is the cycle when you can pursue higher education and make the most of your intelligence. Under the influence of Venus, the ages of thirty-five to forty-two is the cycle when you build your love life. Under the influence of Saturn, the ages of forty-two to forty-nine is the cycle when there are a lot of karmic debts to resolve, because this is a cycle filled with karmic lessons. We can determine what cycle of our lives we are in by calculating our soul code, but there is also a larger pattern of cycles at work that we must take into consideration.

The Pattern of Seven

In the numerological world we live in, the secret to knowing where we are is in understanding and aligning with the pattern of creation—the Pattern of Seven.

According to numerology, the pattern of our world is a pattern of 3, 7, and 12:

* 3 corresponds to the three planes of existence: physical, astral, and divine.

* 7 corresponds to the seven creative planets: the Sun, the Moon, Mars, Mercury, Venus, Jupiter, and Saturn. The seven planets are also the root of the Seventh Seal of Solomon and the Kabala. (The other planets, Uranus, Neptune, and Pluto, were not calculated by the Kabala.)

* 12 corresponds to the twelve signs of the zodiac: The Sun rules Leo, the Moon rules Cancer, Mars rules Aries and Scorpio, Mercury rules Gemini and Virgo, Venus rules Taurus and Libra, Jupiter rules Sagittarius, Saturn rules Capricorn, Uranus rules Aquarius, and Neptune rules Pisces.

The Seven-Year Cycles of Your Life

By looking at your life according to ten distinct periods of time, or the seven-year cycles, you can examine where you are in your life cycle.

Cycle 1. The Sun governs the first cycle of years in your life, from birth to age seven. During this time, you are in the growth process.

Cycle 2. The Moon governs the second set of years, ages seven to fourteen. At this time, the focus is on your emotional life and learning to understand yourself.

Cycle 3. Mars rules the third set of years, fourteen through twenty-one. During these years of adolescence, you struggle to build emotional and physical strength and learn more about your sexuality.

Cycle 4. Mercury rules the cycle of twenty-one through twenty-eight, the period in which you develop rational thought and your belief systems.

Cycle 5. Jupiter, the planet of prosperity, helps you build career and family during the fifth cycle, between ages twenty-eight and thirty-five.

Cycle 6. Venus rules the sixth cycle, between ages thirty-five and forty-two, and encourages you to savor life and truly enjoy it.

Cycle 7. Saturn, which rules the seventh cycle, between ages forty-two and forty-nine, teaches you all the lessons of karma in order to help you develop wisdom.

Cycle 8. The eighth cycle, between ages forty-nine and fifty-six, is influenced by Uranus, the planet of transformation.

Cycle 9. The ninth cycle, between ages fifty-six and sixty-three, is under Neptune, the planet of the metaphysical. Your focus during this time is on spirituality.

Cycle 10. Age sixty-three is the climactic year. This is when you begin to experience the influence of Pluto, the planet of death and transformation. According to calculations and statistics, more people die at sixty-three than at any other age. After seventy, the cycle starts over.

Nine- and Twelve-Year Cycles

Some people may take longer than seven years to go through each of these cycles. For instance, when people are destined to live a longer life, their cycle of evolution and movement between the planets is not necessarily based on a cycle of seven. Instead, it can extend to cycles of nine or even twelve years. Usually, people who have 8 or 9 in their birth number are destined to survive the test of time and will live a longer life.

Now that you have a better understanding of your soul code and the cycles of your life, you're equipped with knowledge about how your life fits into time and space. You have the tools to shape your future. In part II we'll learn how to release blockages that prevent you from engaging your will to co-create your destiny, and I'll share with you stories from some of my clients to illustrate these ideas in action.

You've demystified your soul code; now let's learn how to make the most of it.

PART II

Opening Your Mind

3

Taking Responsibility and Getting Unstuck

Before we move on, it's important to understand the differences among predictions, premonitions, and prophecies. While these terms are sometimes used interchangeably, there are clear distinctions among them.

Predictions. Some predictions are based on calculations, and some are rooted in the sixth sense of the predictor. First, some predictions are based on the traditional tools of the ancient arts, such as astrology and numerology, according to the belief that the entire world is mathematical. Nostradamus, for example, was an expert astrologer and numerologist. All his predictions were based on numbers and his knowledge of these arts. The other type of prediction is based on images and visions in the third eye of the seer. A prediction usually concerns an individual's future.

Premonitions. Premonitions are a sense of upcoming events in dreams or a waking state, such as feeling uneasy or having a gut feeling that tells you something is about to happen. While premonitions are usually related to personal matters, some people can sense natural disasters, such as an earthquake or a volcanic eruption, before they happen.

Prophecies. While predictions and premonitions are more about individuals, a prophecy works on a global scale. A prophecy is a vision or a revelation of a major event of such magnitude that it will affect many people. Prophecy is the anticipation of the manifestation of the collective consciousness. Prophecies come from precognition, or knowledge, of the future. However, not all knowledge of the future becomes a prophecy.

In ancient times, prophecies were made by oracles and were considered unchangeable. Throughout history, religious prophecies were made by so-called Great Spirits, a Great Man or Great Woman choosing to preach a divine message. Buddha, Jesus, and Mohammed were all prophets. The Bible talks about very real prophecies. The Hebrews consulted the Torah and tarot. Muslims believe all people are meant to have prophecies that are given to us as guidance.

Only certain unique souls are appointed by divine energy to make true prophecies; these souls have no karmic ties to the physical world and are considered masters of superior human intelligence.

Beware of false prophets. They can be found everywhere, usually preaching on street corners. False prophets and false psychics are dangerous to your spirit. They prey on your fears and insecurities for gain and tell you nonsense or negative information. A psychic reading should be a positive experience; those who visit psychics should come away from the reading feeling optimistic about the future, even if the psychic predicts challenges ahead.

Taking Responsibility

Jackie

Jackie was in love with her boyfriend for years. When she came to see me, she had just broken up with him. She didn't trust him because he was cheating on her. I told Jackie that her boyfriend was still in love with her and that he would come back. Jackie (born 3/11/1980) has a soul code of 5. As a 5, she is a free spirit who values her freedom. I saw that she needed to learn to forgive and consider the deeper reasons for people being in her life.

The next time I heard from Jackie, she and her boyfriend had indeed gotten back together. She said she was happy and was ready to marry him, but I was concerned that she still didn't trust him. I sensed that she could become insecure and suspicious again. I knew that if she sent out those bad feelings, she could easily ruin the relationship.

A short time later she came back to tell me that they had broken up again. She said that I had been wrong about him, that he was a bad person. But I knew I had been right. Jackie had chosen not to take responsibility for her own negative attitude, and it had prevented her from manifesting a fulfilling relationship.

You can become stuck when you let one of the four main negative emotions—anger, fear, hatred, or jealousy—take over your life. When you are charged with emotion, you spin out of control. You lose touch with your higher self, you are unaware of your intention, you lose your balance, and you become incapable of projecting positive energy or accessing memory. Without self-awareness you can literally self-destruct.

Some people who come to me have been stuck for years. Their relationships, finances, and careers are all stagnant. Often their creative mind hasn't been used in such a long time that they doubt they even have one. They are not growing—they're dying. They are filled with doubt about living out their dreams. Sometimes they even forget they have dreams! But of course we all dream. And more importantly, we all have the power to make our dreams come true.

Gina

The first thing I do with clients is help them understand where they are right now. Unless you understand what cycle of your life you're currently in, it's almost impossible to know where to begin to make changes. I ask my clients soul-searching questions like, "What exactly is it you want to get from your life?" I tell them to think of me as a spiritual coach who can help them evaluate where they are and where they want to be and then help them project that dream into the future.

I also remind them that this is work everyone can continue to do for themselves. Each of us has great power to control our destiny, and with that power comes tremendous responsibility. Only you are responsible for your own life. Yet I find over and over that people refuse to accept this.

Gina comes from a well-established, "old money" family. She has an Ivy League education, a beautiful house, a baby, and financial security, yet she is afraid to make a move without consulting me. She calls me several times a day asking for guidance, and she second-guesses herself. I adore her, but she has completely lost connection with her inner compass. By being so dependent on me, she refuses to accept responsibility for her own life, which is a tragedy.

Jenny

I meet many people who are addicted to what they believe is a "quick fix," a magic answer from a psychic or therapist or an easy solution that someone drops in their lap. Others become trapped in their dependency to those close to them. That was the case with Jenny.

When Jenny came to me, she was confused. She was in a relationship with a man who treated her badly and made her unhappy. Jenny is a 1, born 4/7/1970. Missing a 2 in her code means she will have to work hard in relationships to overcome her difficulty in expressing love and her fear of commitment. Because these traits don't come naturally to her, she is stubborn.

When I asked her why she stayed with him, she said she was afraid to be by herself because she didn't have a job. Then I asked her what her mother was like, and she told me she was domineering and controlling. I explained that this is why she chose this pattern with her boyfriend but that soon she would be offered a choice.

She told me she had already received an offer to go Australia for one year and work in marketing. I advised her to go. I sensed that she would meet someone there from Europe, a tall man with blue eyes who came from a great family.

Instead of being excited, she was full of doubt. What if she went and didn't meet this man? I told her that the man was indeed there and that it was up to her to make the journey. In the end she said she was afraid to go. She was afraid to leave her boyfriend and her mother.

Jenny saw herself as powerless without her mother or boyfriend and was not willing to let that destructive, yet familiar, pattern go. As long as she continued to perceive herself as a victim of her life circumstances and relationships, that's exactly what she would be.

Only you can truly know what is right for you. Putting your life in the hands of shrinks, personal coaches, your parents, or your spouse will not fulfill your dreams. Trust yourself and take charge of your future.

The Missing Piece of the Cosmic Puzzle: Personal Action

Donna

My client Donna was worried about her roommate and friend, Tina, who had lost her job and was feeling vulnerable and afraid. Tina joined a church group, which appeared to be a positive move, but over time Donna became concerned. Instead of looking for a job, Tina spent all her time passing out flyers and trying to recruit people to join the church. Whenever Donna asked Tina what she was doing about finding a job, Tina would simply say, "God will provide." A month went by and Tina still wasn't able to pay the rent. Finally Donna found out that none of the church members had jobs. The church leader told them that they didn't need to look for work, that "God will provide."

Tina had not only fallen into a potentially dangerous cult, but she was also subscribing to a common misconception, that putting all your faith in God, or what I call the Invisible World, means you don't have to do any work for yourself. I believe that the Universe is abundant and that if you put your faith in the Invisible World, it will provide what you need. But Tina was missing an essential piece to the cosmic puzzle: her own participation. The Invisible World will provide only if you are proactive. For Tina, that would mean sending out résumés and going on interviews.

Donna wanted to know what the future had in store for her and Tina. Would Tina be able to find a job and pay her share of the rent, or would Donna eventually be forced to ask her to move out? I told her that Tina's future was in Tina's hands. But as her friend, it was Donna's job to help her see that she must take action and that being passive or feeling like a victim would only perpetuate her jobless situation. Donna's other task was to accept responsibility for her own situation: God was not going to swoop down and drop the rent money into Tina's purse if Tina remained unemployed. Donna needed to make sure the rent would be paid, no matter what Tina chose for herself.

When you act helpless and refuse to take responsibility for yourself, the Invisible World will act in kind. When you take action and show up for yourself, the Invisible World will support your efforts and your willingness to become more aware and to connect with the Divine.

Annette

Sometimes we miss our destiny when we fail to act and when the will is not engaged. Annette was forty-three and wanted to know if she would ever get married. Annette is a 9, born 9/2/1960. Missing the 6 in her code means she has to actively work on family, loving, and being loved.

I told her that she was more ready now than ever. She asked me if I was getting a name, and the name that came to me was Daniel. She couldn't believe it. Three years earlier she had had a session with Sylvia Brown, who told her she would marry a man named Daniel, but nothing had happened. Then she called a woman in Arizona who told her the same thing. "Where is this guy?" she asked. Rather than demanding an answer, that's a question she could have used to inspire her quest to find him.

How is it that she received the same message for three years about the same man from three different sources, and still she couldn't attract what was meant to be? Annette was expecting Daniel to magically appear in her life, without taking any initiatives, without asking her higher self to guide her, or without tuning in to signals and signs as to how their paths may cross.

When Predictions Don't Come True

Predictions open your mind to new opportunities, but it is crucial that you participate in the creation of your own future. Nothing in the world comes without effort; things don't just happen by themselves. I may predict that you will write a book, but unless you do the hard work required to write that book, it won't happen. You may be meant to write a book, you may have important things to say, or you may be a gifted writer, but my prediction isn't enough; you must do the work or that prediction will be blocked.

Sometimes it's clear when predictions don't come true that we are allowing our fears to block us, as in Jenny's case. Other times it's not as obvious, as in Helen's.

Helen

Ten months after I did a session for Helen, she called and reminded me that I had predicted that she would have a healthy baby boy during the summer of 2005. She did, in fact, become pregnant in the very month I had said she would. But there was a problem with the pregnancy. The baby had a serious chromosomal problem called trisomy 18, and Helen had to terminate the pregnancy.

She wondered what had gone wrong, because everything happened as I had predicted, only the baby was not healthy. She asked if there was any chance for her to have another baby in the future.

Predictions "go wrong" sometimes because we have mixed feelings about them, choose not to work on them, or decide they're not where we want our energy and focus to go. After all, predictions don't come from the channel or psychic—they are energetic readings of potentiality, of your dreams. They will come true to the degree of energy and conscious desire you invest in them. If you hold an unconscious contrary wish or fear, it will inevitably work against you.

Perhaps Helen had mixed feelings about being a mother, or perhaps the child I saw for her is still to come. As an 8, born 5/3/1980, she is romantic but has a lot of karma to resolve in this life. Missing the 2 in her code means the lesson of being a mother is a hard one.

Valerie

I always read the audience when I present at seminars. One night I noticed a beautiful woman named Valerie in the back, and I saw that she would become pregnant and have a boy. After the show I told Valerie that she would have a son who would look like her and that she would name him after her grandfather, who had died recently. She said that she had broken up with her boyfriend two months ago and couldn't see how it would be possible. She was clearly hurt by their breakup. I told her that her boyfriend would return to her and that they would be married.

A short time later, she called to tell me that they indeed had gotten back together. The prediction had opened her to forgiveness and to accept her boyfriend back into her life. When I heard from her again, she told me that they had gotten married and were expecting but that I was wrong about the baby—it was a girl.

Three years later I heard from Valerie again. She had just given birth to a baby boy, whom she named after her grandfather. She had taken the prediction to heart and made it manifest, but the heart often has its own timing.

Working with Nonbelievers

Resistance to change takes many forms. For some clients I have seen, it's a kind of game that they are "difficult" and can't be helped. In a way, they are exhibiting a form of arrogance underneath that is actually fear—the fear of exposure and of claiming their own connection with the Divine.

One day I got a call from a woman in Canada. She told me that she was sick and needed help but that she did not believe anyone could read her. "No one ever has been right about me," she said.

OK, I said to myself, it is going to be difficult to convince her. I asked if she was separated. No, she said. Did she have two children? No. Was she divorced? No.

"I told you this is not going to work," she said. "You don't know anything about me."

Then I asked her who had died of a heart attack and who Robert was.

She said her husband had died of a heart attack, and Robert was the name of one of her sons. I asked if she had two sons. She said that she had three.

She said that she felt like she had poison in her body and that her left leg was very bad. I told her that I didn't see any of this and that she was not sick. Then I asked her who was going to jail. She said she didn't know.

I told her that she did know, that I saw a lawsuit, and that someone who had worked with her husband would go to jail. With that, I broke through her resistance. She asked to have a session with me in person.

It is possible to make a real connection, even with a nonbeliever.

4

Working with Predictions

Once you take responsibility for your future and engage your heart and your mind, anything is possible. Opening your mind begins with changing your perceptions: how you see yourself and the circumstances of your life. As Einstein said, we live "in the world of possibilities."

We all love possibilities. But when we refuse to accept an alternative reality presented to us, we can actually keep it from happening. The first step in tapping into the power of your mind is opening up to the unknown, to the realm of infinite possibilities. Predictions are readings of future possibilities. We have a choice about whether we want that future or not.

The mind is constantly predicting information. It sends us signals every minute of our lives, but we tend to ignore them. How can we become more aware and stop depending on what others see for us and start seeing for ourselves? How do we transform our negative thoughts and projections into positive ones? How do we open our minds and make the most of the predictions and insights we receive and project our future?

First we start with intentions that we put into play with our actions. In other words, start with a plan of what you intend to do and then work hard to get the results of what you want to accomplish. Doing so will put us on a more positive path toward our future.

I receive calls from all over the world, but I was surprised when I heard from Alexandria, who was serving in the Iraq war. Alexandria is a 7, born 8/1/1978. This makes her wise, spiritual, and a deep thinker. Missing the 9 from her code makes her get involved in work for the greater good and bring peace and hope to others. She had many fears and concerns about her well-being, her mission there, and her position as a hospital corpsman. She also wanted to know if her relationship with her boyfriend at home would survive her long absence. In our session, I told her that nursing was indeed part of her destiny and that she would make a good pediatric nurse. I also reassured her that her relationship was strong.

After our session, she wrote, "I want to thank you for reminding me that nursing is part of my destiny. Like you said, I also have to stick to my dreams and let my new command know why I feel I should become a hospital corpsman. You also were right about Rusty being my soul mate. Despite the long distance, he and I have remained close, and he still wants to marry me. Your reading gave me hope for the future."

Alexandria's willingness to work with her future possibilities aligned her with her destiny.

For Jen, working with her prediction not only helped her make the right choices for her physical well-being but also brought the joy of a dream fulfilled. She wrote:

"For three years I suffered from an illness that no one could figure out. Prior to the illness I was in the fitness industry, a competitor, the essence of health. I saw many doctors and underwent many tests, but no one could diagnose what was wrong with me. Finally I was told I had chronic fatigue syndrome.

"Each day was a struggle. I suffered in hope that the next day would be better. I was thirty years old and felt discouraged, angry, and helpless. I knew this wasn't living. My husband and I had dreamt of having children someday. Then we went to see you, and you told me that my health was fine but that I just had a thyroid disorder which could be healed. I had taken thyroid tests many times before, but nothing had ever been detected.

"A few weeks later I went to a new doctor. He said, 'You have a thyroid problem, but it's not detected on the blood tests.' Today my health is great, and I feel like a new person. And . . . I'm five months pregnant with twins! I'm grateful for the insights you have given me to understand life and shift the energy in me."

The Timing of Predictions

Timing and locating when a prediction will happen in the physical world is the most difficult part of predicting. Predictions come from the nonphysical world, where time does not exist. Also, our reality is not fixed but is shifting and changing all the time with every action we take.

Five hundred years ago, Nostradamus spoke of 1999 between July and September as being one of the most difficult times of history. He said that war would result. He spoke of the conflicts in the Middle East and about the "twin brothers" being hit. Years later, it all happened.

In January 1999 I was invited to appear on *Good Day New York*. I was asked many questions about what would happen in the coming year. I made a lot of predictions on that show: Russia will have a new leader; the pope will die after Easter; the United States will go to war with Iraq and will eliminate Saddam Hussein; we will go to Mars and discover water; and Clinton will not be impeached. As it turned out, some of the predictions I saw back then took six years to happen, but they all did come true.

During my book tour in 2002, I was interviewed at station KLM in California. One of the many questions I was asked was whether Jennifer Aniston and Brad Pitt would be having a baby. I said that I didn't see a baby and that their relationship would unfortunately not last for more than three years. Three years later their separation was all the news.

A prediction you sense may take years to come true. Before then it might feel like nothing is happening. You might not even remember your prediction. But if you have opened yourself to its possibility, your prediction is working nonetheless.

Predictions That Open the Heart

Tiziana called me from Japan. She had lost family members and was overwhelmed with feelings of grief and loneliness.

She had questions about finding the remaining members of her family. Her desire to connect with them was mixed with doubt and fear. After her session, she wrote:

"When you told me that my karma with my family was not yet resolved and when you gave me a specific name, something clicked in my head and I realized that I had to track down some people I hadn't seen in twenty-five years.

"Well, not only did I find them, but they all welcomed me with open arms and hearts. Our reunion was fantastic. I shall never forget how I felt in their company. I have found some answers, and above all, I have discovered the love of a real family, [which is] a totally new feeling for me."

Tiziana is a 4, born 2/1/1972. She is generous and loving. Missing the 8 from her soul code is why she had to work so hard to resolve her family karma. Interestingly, she was in a personal year 8 when she made all this happen. That is the year for resolving family karma and for looking for a new life and a new you. You don't have this chance many times in a lifetime.

The key to Tiziana's healing was her courage to act on the information she received with an open heart. Receiving information with an open heart can take many forms. Some of my clients tape our sessions so that they can revisit the information I've given them and use it as positive reinforcement. They often meditate on what was revealed in their reading so they can explore the range of feelings it provokes in them at their own pace. Meditating on the information also assists them in making additional discoveries about their true wishes and desires and helps them tune in to their own inner compass.

Synchronicity: What Is Meant to Be

There is a major difference between working on your predictions and the events in your life you have control over and dealing with destined events that happen unexpectedly. Predictions require action; destiny requires surrender and acceptance.

One day one of my best friends invited me to her birthday party. Out of habit I asked myself why I was there, other than being there for my friend. For me, there is always a reason inside a reason.

I was just about to leave the party when a man came in, apologizing for being so late, and sat down next to me. I turned to him and said, "You'll be moving from where you live. You'll be forced to."

He got upset and raised his voice: "How dare you comment on my life and what I have to do? This is unacceptable behavior. Please don't talk to me!"

I felt terrible. I apologized and didn't say another word. I told myself that I would never again give information without being asked. A half hour later, the man approached me and said, "I don't know you, but you're right. I do have to move from my home and find another place. Coming here to this party, I never expected anything like this would happen."

His name was Jonathan and he was a psychic from New Mexico. We established a great connection that day. I felt he was the reason I was at that party, though it wasn't clear to me exactly why. Two weeks later I had my answer: Victoria, my producer, asked me if I knew of a male psychic for a television show.

Synchronicity is when events that are meant to be coincide with events that are meant to play a part in your life. But when something is meant to be, you must do the work to know why. Everything that is meant to be must make sense to you. Every person who comes into your life is meant to be there. Your work is to know why, what they have to show you, and how you can make the most of your coming together. Synchronicity is proof that we are on our chosen path and that we are listening, and the more we listen and go with the flow, the more help we receive from the Invisible World.

Choosing to Heal

What is meant to be is intricately linked with your past and to the karma that you have to resolve in this lifetime. It was your destiny to be born on a certain date, into a certain family, and with specific physical aspects, a specific genetic code, and distinguished skills, strengths, and weaknesses. But the choices you make in your life are the work of your free will. Your free will is at work when you analyze what is best for you, set intentions, and then put those intentions to work. By ignoring your free will, you invite pain, suffering, and stagnation. In exercising your free will, you hold an incredible power to choose from the myriad options that life has to offer and to transform suffering into joy.

Dorie's strong use of free will and her firm belief in my prediction that she would live a long life got her through a major physical crisis. Dorie is a remarkable woman from Sweden who has come to visit me many times. She has become a dear friend. She has a Ph.D. in biopsychology and is helping the world better understand the complex workings of the criminal mind. In 2004 she had a health crisis. Her body stopped producing insulin, she suffered from terrible itching, and she had pain in many of her organs. The doctors first said she had diabetes. She went to the hospital for treatment and tests. Then they told her that the diabetes diagnosis was wrong and, worse yet, that she had cancer in her gall bladder which would require radical surgery and would put her life in danger.

When she called me she was shocked and confused. I told her that I did not believe she had cancer. She didn't believe she had cancer either, but the tests showed otherwise. Without an operation she would have only six months to live. I told her she would live a long life, and I worked with her every week to give her support and build her trust. During that time I recommended a healer in Boston named Jon Sweeney, who works with Coherence Therapy over the phone. Coherence Therapy is a healing modality that Jon developed, inspired by Ton Ren/Chi Gong healing. It honors the knowledge of both Western and traditional Chinese medicine, and it uses the nonlocality principle of quantum physics to effect change in physical health. Coherence Therapy heals the body on a cellular level.

Working with Dorie, Jon found a growth around her bile duct, but he did not feel it was cancerous. Dorie decided to ask her doctor for a second opinion. While the tests were inconclusive, the doctor still recommended radical surgery that would leave Dorie in a semi-invalid state. Despite this information, Dorie was convinced that she did not have cancer. She understood the consequences of waiting but was willing to accept the risks. She and Jon worked on a weekly basis while her doctors continued their tests. Finally the tests showed that she did have a problem with her gall bladder but that there was no cancer. Dorie continued to work on her healing and regained her strength. Less than five months later, she returned to work.

As a 3, born 8/9/1948, Dorie is powerful and creative. Because she is missing 7, the planet of spirituality, she will have lessons in seeking and contemplating the mysteries of life and death over her lifetime. Having an 8 in her code means she will live for a long time and overcome diseases. Dorie was in a personal year 9—a year for collecting past karma and letting go of the past—when her health crisis and healing occurred.

Dorie's willingness to work with Jon Sweeney and with me was due to her willingness to participate in her own healing. We can make use of all that is available to us—integrating all healing modalities—to promote our well-being. We can learn to use consciousness to change our physical aspects.

Mind over Matter

Evolutionary healing methods such as Coherence Therapy and Therapeutic Touch are based in the theory of "mind over matter." Esoteric and spiritual teachers have known for ages that each cell in our body is shaped and programmed by the words we speak and by our thoughts. Our body is not only programmed by our genes but also by our thoughts: You become what you think. Language has a tremendous impact on the body, and living tissue can react to language, which explains the power of affirmations on our physical being.

Science has uncovered evidence that our DNA can be influenced and reprogrammed by words and sound frequencies without cutting out or replacing a single gene. This has profound implications for human potential. As we become more aware of how to manipulate our genetic code, we can eradicate the code of diseases and problems that we genetically inherit. We can reprogram ourselves to live in health and wholeness.

The power of mind over matter is the realization that words form frequencies that can change our genetic makeup. Ninety percent of our genetic code can actually be shifted by the power of our thoughts. The more conscious your thought process, the greater power you have to transform yourself from the inside out.

Individuals must work on their inner process and development in order to establish a conscious communication with their DNA. In order to do that we first must acknowledge our higher self as our "higher frequency." Then we can use the tools of accessing the higher mind, through meditation and relaxation, to open the pathways for our higher self and our physical self to work together. (See chapters 9 and 10.)

Opening the mind is an amazing process of evolution. When you open your mind to a new belief, you begin the process of changing your genetic coding, which will bring healing and change.

5

The Power Within:
Reprogram Your Thoughts,
Reprogram Your Mind

Is the incurable always incurable?

Carol has Graves' disease, a failure of the thyroid gland that causes extreme pain throughout the body, especially in the eyes, where the result is a bulging effect. Many people, including former first lady Barbara Bush, suffer from this incurable disease. When Carol came to me several years ago, I knew she could be helped and recommended that she work with Jon Sweeney.

Carol was skeptical. She couldn't believe that talking to a person on the telephone could have any impact on her physical health. Nonetheless, she began working with him. During their first session, Carol failed to mention to Jon that she had injured her shoulder at the gym, but Jon told her right away that there was a problem with her left shoulder and that he would fix it. The pain went away almost instantly. Carol was now ready to accept that further healing was possible. She continued her sessions with Jon, which included Jon reading the energy of her disease and sending energy and instructions for change directly to the affected area.

During the weeks of treatment, Carol noticed that her pain began to disappear and that her bulging eyes resumed a normal appearance. She decided she wanted to stop taking the medication, which had limited effectiveness and caused unpleasant side effects. With her doctor's help, she gradually reduced her medication. Not only did her disease remain dormant, but her health and energy also improved. Carol has been off her medication for nearly two years. Her blood work is normal, and she has noticed an improvement in her memory and her ability to focus.

At first, Carol wondered if there would be any side effects to Jon's work, and there are. Carol is naturally capable, competent, and professional, and she now has the energy to meet the demands of her growing small business and the emotional well-being necessary to cope with its challenges. She also enjoys robust health. The need to treat the disease on a weekly basis has long passed. Carol chooses to work with Jon on the phone once a week because of the positive side effects. Their sessions now focus on prevention and enhancement. Like the others with whom Jon works, he and Carol have never met.

Carol's dramatic recovery forces us to rethink the limitations of traditional medical practices and the mind's ability to reprogram the body. Despite her severe diagnosis and her own initial doubts, Carol's willingness to work with Jon has helped her to change her way of thinking about her disease, unlocking her body's ability to heal. Jon's work causes us to rethink the boundaries of medicine and the ability of the mind.

Once we acknowledge that we have the power of the mind to literally heal ourselves from the inside out, it becomes our job to be conscious of our thoughts and to "rewire" ourselves for constructive patterns of thinking. The mind is like a computer that needs to be constantly programmed with correct information. But if you program your mind with confusing or incorrect information, you will get a confused life.

Every day a million thoughts go through your brain, and each one affects your health, your peace of mind, your relationships, and your overall well-being. Everything you think has the potential to translate into reality. There are things you can control and things you can't, but the most important thing you have control over is your own thoughts. So why not utilize that control every minute of your life and reprogram your mind with positive information and positive energy?

With all that's at stake, it's extremely important to know where you are in your life and to know that you are going in the right direction. Your thoughts attract certain events. The better you know yourself and the more aware you are of what is right for you, the better you are able to recognize events as either good opportunities or ones you should avoid.

Developing Awareness of Your Thoughts and Beliefs

Most of the time we are unaware of our thinking process. Instead we cling to old beliefs and conditioning learned years ago from our families, religious instruction, and education. These beliefs may have served us while we were growing up and learning how to survive in the physical world, but they fall short when it comes to developing our multidimensional higher powers.

As children, we are told many things; we are given social laws and rules of conduct to abide by. We are punished if we don't obey the rules and trained to believe that our life is a series of fixed sequential events: going to school, integrating into society, getting married, having children, and basically doing what others do.

At the same time, we experience inner resistance to following all these dos and don'ts. Feeling lost, depressed, frustrated, powerless, and enraged are all signs of our inner resistance to outer oppression or limiting beliefs. These feelings are warning signals from our subconscious that it's time for a change.

From the time she was young, Larissa's family wanted her to go to law school. They convinced her that it was a great way to make money, so she studied hard, went to law school, earned her degree, and eventually landed a job at a law firm. Her mother had also convinced her that she must marry a Catholic, warning her that otherwise her father wouldn't approve. Larissa did what she was told and married a man from a nice Catholic family. For years, she went through the motions of this life based on others' expectations. Then it all came crashing down.

When Larissa came in for counseling, she was sad and disappointed. She was thirty-seven and divorced, and she had no idea what she wanted or what to do next. Doing what was expected of her, Larissa had given away her power and failed to develop her self-awareness. She had lost her connection to her inner voice and with it her ability to trust her own decisions.

Larissa was born 8/2/1963, making her a 2. She is an intelligent and quiet person. She was born into a family where there was criticism and control, and as a result, she grew up with low self-confidence and low self-esteem. Missing the 5, 6, and 7 is part of the reason she had problems in her relationships with her father and her husband. Missing these numbers also will present more lessons in this life that she will have to learn the hard way.

Determining Your Level of Consciousness

I have developed two exercises that work together to help you wake up and determine where you are in your level of consciousness.

The first exercise, "Fulfilling the Higher Self," focuses on your inner, or spiritual, life and the needs of your soul. This list of questions is designed to help you pinpoint your soul's needs and understand what brings you fulfillment. From there, you can begin to evaluate your goals.

The second, "Fulfilling the Physical Self," provides specific questions to help you evaluate the conditions of your material life, such as whether you are living in the right place, if you are in a suitable career, and if you have helpful people around you. The key here is that your spiritual growth is not separate from your physical well-being but depends on it. You cannot fulfill the callings of your soul if your physical life is full of suffering and chaos.

Take time to contemplate the following questions and then make a list of your answers.

Exercises in Evolution

Are your spiritual self and physical self in harmony?

Fulfilling the Higher Self

* How well do you know the spiritual you?

* Do you take time to sit, meditate, and listen for inner guidance?

* Do you listen to your thoughts and feelings?

* What are your beliefs?

* Do you believe in the life of the soul?

* Do you know your spiritual guides?

* What is your Higher Self looking for?

* Do you fulfill your dreams?

Fulfilling the Physical Self

∗ Are you happy with the condition of your health?

∗ Do you have the energy and vitality to do what you enjoy?

∗ Are you happy with your physical appearance?

∗ Are you happy in your home?

∗ Do you feel you are in the right career?

∗ Do the people in your life provide you with physical and emotional support and intellectual stimulation?

Review your answers to determine how well your physical reality is supporting your soul's needs and requirements. For example, if one of the needs of your Higher Self is to be a part of a supportive creative community, but you are isolated or surrounded by people who have addictive or negative patterns, the two are in conflict. If your answer to any of the questions in this section is no, ask yourself, "What am I willing to change?" or "How can I choose differently?" If there are strong discrepancies between your spiritual needs and your physical reality, you will remain blocked and unhappy and fail to reach the next level in your spiritual evolution.

Trusting Your Own Abilities

In order to trust yourself, it's important to be in touch with your needs, your skills, and your abilities to make your own decisions. Here is a list of guidelines for building self-trust.

* Make your own decisions. The day you make your first decision is the day you learn your first lesson of life.

* Never stagnate and never give up on your dream. Once you have a plan, stay with it and don't let anyone discourage you.

* Trust that you know better than anyone else what is best for you.

* You will experience some bumps on your way, but keep going.

* We belong to God, so don't confine your happiness to what is on Earth.

* Don't try to build too many castles; what they offer you does not last. Instead, build a healthy body, mind, and spirit; build your peace.

* Enjoy life; it's so beautiful. Stay in the light of life and find balance.

6

Tuning In: Working with Premonitions, Dreams, and Messages

Walking down the street, you may suddenly feel something come over you, a sense that something is about to happen—a "gut" feeling. That's a premonition. A premonition is an early warning of future events and is dominated by physical sensations: an inexplicable feeling of unease or excitement that something bad or good is about to happen. Feelings of unexplained and sudden fear, anxiety, or depression often come before a death or an accident. Similarly, feelings of joy for no apparent reason can presage our good fortune, such as meeting our soul mate or being in the right place at the right time. We all have the ability to receive premonitions, but many times we ignore them.

Premonitions offer us proof of our intuitive abilities, which come from the part of the mind that knows where our life is headed. Because we all view the world through a different lens, the degree to which we receive premonitions depends on our level of perception. We can receive premonitions when we are awake, through signs and signals from others or ourselves, or through our dreams. By training yourself to listen for these signs you can alter the game plan: you can prevent the accident or misfortune from happening, or in the case of good news, you can be ready and willing to say yes.

Recurring Dreams

When premonitions come during our dream state, they are usually coded with symbols and metaphors we have to interpret. Recurring dreams offer us an unusual opportunity to decode a message that is repeatedly trying to break through to our awareness.

Rebecca had a recurring dream that she was married to a man she did not know. She was in a small church dressed in white, and there was a tall man with brown hair smiling at her, ready to marry her. She wondered what this dream meant to show her or if it was just wishful thinking on her part.

To work with a repetitive dream, replay the whole dream and then break it down into symbols. You can look at the symbols as metaphors for your state of mind. For example, water indicates emotions, and cloudy water shows there is something to be cleared or released in your emotions. Fire might indicate burning rage, desire, or alchemical transformation. Keeping a dream journal is helpful in deciphering your dreams. You can also find more information about dream symbols in numerous books and on the Internet.

What we wish for ourselves always comes true. Dreams can also show us unconscious wishes. Rebecca's dream could be interpreted in several ways. On one level, the smiling man in her dream could be showing her that there is clearly a part of her which is willing to invite a partner into her life, especially one who is ready and available. Symbolically, the man could represent the masculine side of her personality that is ready to show up and make commitments. The fact that the man is a stranger could indicate she has some work to do to get to know that side of herself.

Sometimes a dream is a projection of the soul's battle of good versus evil or light over the dark during a time of intense spiritual growth. For most of his life, Chris had experienced intense struggle and hardship. He had a dream that included images of the Blessed Mother and what he felt was evil incarnate:

"It was then I felt myself flying into the other room. To me, it felt as though I was swirling down a spiral staircase with one hand clasped around the center support pole. My feet never touched a single stair; when I reached the other room, I found myself staring at an evil presence. Curiously, the shape this evil took was that of a young girl in a frilly dress yellowed with age. The presence was facing and directing its evil energy toward another young girl who was wearing the same frilly dress—yet this dress was pristine and colored in the purest white. I could feel the chill of fear flowing over my entire body and struggled to speak. It was a sense of fear that nearly took my breath away. Without saying a word, I prayed to Jesus in my head, asking for his help. It was then that the words spilled from my mouth, 'Demon, get out of my house!' At that, the young girl in the tarnished dress immediately scampered toward the door, opened it, and ran out. Somehow I choked out, 'And never come back!'

"I woke with a start, with the intense imagery still quite fresh in my mind. At that very moment, I heard birds chirping outside my bedroom window, but then I realized it was only 1:12 A.M. 'Birds don't typically chirp that early,'

I thought. 'Could it be?' Though I cannot be sure, the chirping comforted me immediately, and thoughts of the Blessed Mother filled my head."

Looking at Chris's dream, the image of the young girls can be seen as the innocent and feminine, or receptive, part of Chris that had to battle for its survival, while birds are often seen as the messengers of Spirit. The dream showed Chris that he had won this profound battle on the deepest level of his soul and that it was what he later called "a test of faith." For Chris, that faith included faith in himself and in his own ability to heal.

Healing Fears, Phobias, and Addictions

Dreams demonstrate the mind's amazing ability to work with the subconscious to heal emotional wounds. When subconscious fears appear in our waking life, however, they come as phobias and addictions, and we need to ask for help to clear them.

Lizy was terrified of driving a car because of her fear of being killed in a car accident. When she came for a session, she wanted to know how she could get rid of her phobia. Using hypnotherapy, we did a regression, and she was able to vividly recall details of an accident she had experienced. By accessing that memory, Lizy was able to release the emotional memory held in her body and cellular memory. Once that energy was released, the fear her mind associated with it was able to subside and eventually to disappear.

Phobias and negative impressions that come from past experiences are stored in the right hemisphere of the brain. By using regression techniques such as hypnotherapy, you can erase the memory held in the cells that trigger the phobia.

One client had a desperate fear of flying. He had to fly for his job, and the phobia was debilitating. For the first twenty minutes of takeoff, he would become physically sick; he would shake and break out in a sweat and have to grab onto the hand of the person next to him. Once he got through that first twenty minutes, he could fly for hours.

In a hypnotherapy session, he recalled a memory from a previous life during World War II. He was in a plane that had crashed during the first twenty minutes of takeoff. When he recalled the memory, all the symptoms of his phobia surfaced; his face changed, he started shaking, and he broke out in a sweat. He was terrified because he saw himself dying. Each time he relived the event on a plane, he activated those memories. Once he had released this past-life memory, he was able to fly without trauma.

Accessing these memories by building a bridge to the subconscious is the only way we can heal these deep fears. Hypnotherapy is one of the most effective tools there is for helping the mind create that bridge. It can also help release patterns of physical addictions, such as drinking and smoking. The power of hypnotherapy is the power of the mind revealed: its remarkable ability to heal and reprogram itself. Just as we can reprogram a computer, we can erase destructive patterning by rearranging and replacing the old codes with the new.

Mediumship: Receiving Messages from the Other Side

Death takes what the man would keep
and leaves what the man would lose.

PROVERB

When we look at the bigger picture, death is simply the next great adventure. Death is not the end of life. Life flows until it emerges in the eternal.

When the soul enters the body, we call it birth. When the soul leaves the body, we call it death. But the supreme soul is deathless, timeless, causeless, and nonphysical. Death is of the physical body, which is composed of five elements of the material world—earth, water, fire, air, and the auric field, which is the etheric field. If you wish to free yourself from birth and death, you must become bodiless, that is, non-physical. Having a physical body is the result of karma.

Today there is growing interest in mediums and communicating with the dead. This is because we have entered the Age of Aquarius, and people are seeking to achieve a higher consciousness.

Connecting with loved ones on the other side sets in motion a powerful shift in our consciousness and in our perception. We are suddenly willing to see things differently and to open our hearts to the Invisible World. It changes us forever.

The spirits are not in the lower level of consciousness but in the fifth dimension, and they surround us all the time. When we connect with them at this level, we don't see them with our two eyes, but once we detach from our physical environment, we can sense them.

The more we increase our level of perception, the more we are able to receive messages from the fifth dimension. Increasing our level of perception means knowing that the world around us is not everything. There is a parallel, invisible world. The more you go beyond linear time and beyond everyday consciousness, the more you increase your level of perception. You can do this in dreams, hypnosis, and very deep meditation. Souls that are not incarnated—souls we call Spirit guides—exist beyond the four levels of creation and will try to connect and communicate with us. They usually make a connection via the electromagnetic field, which they can usually tap into. They can turn on the TV or switch the lights on or off, which is why we often have funny experiences with lights or electrical appliances when loved ones are trying to connect with us. They can also reach us in other ways through our energy field and shift our perception through a sign or a vision.

The more detached your mind is from the physical world, the easier it is to receive these messages. Souls often come to us in our sleep because we are more relaxed and not trapped in the sensory Universe. Being in that deep state of relaxation, a trance state, or hypnosis, the mind is most open to the possibility of seeing through the veils of physical reality.

Communicating in this way is not only helpful for our soul's evolution, but it's also helpful for those with whom we are connecting. Many times souls can have difficulty evolving after death when those they have left behind are hanging on to intense feelings, such as anger and grief, over their loss. Establishing a connection becomes a powerful way to move through the grieving process and heal.

To open yourself to messages, sit where you will not be disturbed. Breathe deeply as you begin to detach from the physical world. Call to the loved one you wish to connect with. Open your perception to receive his or her message. Your loved one may come right away or in your dreams that night, or he or she may show you a sign.

Catalina

Catalina came to see me from Holland. As I handed her a glass of water, I saw a young woman behind her. I asked her if anyone in her family had died young. She said, yes, her sister died three years ago. I told her that she was there with us and that a man was also with her. He had the initial M and had died after her sister did. Catalina then told me that her father's name began with M and that he had died six months after her sister did. Her sister spoke of a little girl. Catalina said yes, she has a daughter.

The sister continued to speak to me clearly. She told me that Catalina would marry a man from Greece who would come into her life from another time. Catalina said that her boyfriend was from Greece and that they got along well. Her sister went on to say that their mother had a thyroid problem and should change her medication. The session went on with her sister bringing Catalina many messages.

There is no linear time on the other side. Those who have passed on can be present with us, see us, and guide us. But you have to believe.

Mary

I've known Mary for many years. She recently called me in tears to tell me her father had died. The pain of the loss was so great that she couldn't cope. She asked me if I could help. I told her to come to my office and we'd talk to him.

During her session, her father came and appeared very happy. He spoke about himself and the family. He mentioned the names Scott and Kathy. Mary confirmed that he had a sister named Kathy who had a son named Scott. Her father said that Scott had liver problems; Mary said that he had a drinking problem. Then he mentioned a big watch and a ring that he had given Mary's mother. Mary told me that he had given them to her the week before he died, as if he had known he would die. He said to tell Mary that he had indeed known this.

He also said that he would soon show Mary a sign. One week later, Mary sent me a picture of a candle that had been moved from its place and melted. Her father had also told me that he was going to move a painting on her mother's wall, which he did. Mary's connection with her father, knowing he was still with her in spirit, was a tremendous consolation.

Shelly

For Shelly, her connection with the other side reconnected her to a family she had forgotten and healed a wound she had buried. She wrote:

"The first time I spoke with you, you asked me if my dad had died suddenly. I replied, 'No.' You said a man was sitting next to you, smiling and pointing to the letter 'J.' I assumed it was my son, Joey. Then you said he was pointing to the month of January. You said my dad had died suddenly and at a young age. I really thought you were talking about my stepdad, who had died after being sick for many years, but that had nothing to do with January. I didn't pick up on any of this until I got home and told my husband, and he said, 'Shelly, she's talking about Jack—your dad!' I couldn't believe it. I had put him in the back of my mind many years ago. You see, I didn't know Jack was my biological father until I was thirty-five. It was so devastating to me. I deeply loved the man who [had] raised me and didn't want to believe anything different. It was a long story that my stepdad and my mom eventually told me.

"I had only met Jack once, though I will never forget it. He and his wife came to visit my family and me for two weeks. I loved him upon meeting him. I thought how lucky I was to have two dads. He had never been sick, ever. Then one day he was drinking a cup of coffee and died instantly. He was sixty-two or sixty-three. It was the month of January. I was hurt that his family never kept in touch with me, so I put him in the back on my mind to lessen the pain.

"When you told me that he said he [had done] the best he could and [that] he loves me very much, I felt comforted. It all makes sense to me now. I'm glad I finally learned this, as this is important. Your insights and gifts are a blessing to me."

In fact, it was Shelly's willingness to open her heart that brought her this blessing.

Barbara

Sometimes it takes a while to accept our destiny and to receive the messages waiting for us. Barbara wrote:

"The last time you read for me, about five months ago, you said a dear friend who died in a tragic accident, maybe a car accident, was trying to reach me and was always around me. I told you I had no such friend who died in such a manner. Neither of us could figure it out, so you just went on with the reading and I forgot about it.

"Tonight I met up with an old friend whom I haven't seen since our dear mutual friend Patrick passed away from what I thought was AIDS. Well, as it turns out, Patrick died in Paris, but not from AIDS, even though he was suffering from the disease, but in an accident. That is who you were seeing around me—my sweet Patrick. I hope he is at peace now and still enjoys laughing at my seriousness in life."

Knowing that her dear friend was around her eased the tragedy surrounding his death and opened Barbara's ability to connect with him on the other side.

Healing the Soul

When we talk about the soul, there are actually two souls: the individual soul, or the human soul, and the Supreme Soul. The individual soul is a reflection of the Supreme Soul. The Supreme Soul is spirit. It is nonphysical; it is intelligence and consciousness. The individual soul, however, can become impure through the four needs of the ego: pride, selfishness, jealousy, and greed.

Living in the body means we cannot grow beyond our karma—our physical bonds and attachments. When it's time to go, we may feel reluctant to surrender our possessions and surroundings. Death becomes a necessity to heal the soul, not only for those who pass on but for those left behind.

That was the case with Brandy and Sam. Brandy lost her husband, Sam, in the September 11 attack on the World Trade Center. She was eight months pregnant at the time. I counseled her in the weeks and months that followed. Although it was a tragedy, it was also Sam's destiny. He knew he was going to die; six months before the disaster, he took out a life insurance policy for a half-million dollars. Brandy and Sam were truly soul partners, but they were destined to have only a short life together. We've channeled Sam in her sessions. He gives Brandy many wonderful messages about her future. Brandy is taking care of herself and their three children; she has chosen to make peace with her fate.

Those who don't believe in the soul want proof; they need to see to believe. But the soul is not an object of perception. The soul exists beyond the realm of material science.

Purify your soul throughout your life by steering clear of the ego's needs—pride, selfishness, jealousy, and greed—and setting your intentions to connect with the Supreme Soul. Meditate to realize your divine essence. This is the path to immortality.

7

The Power of Perception and Free Will: Reality Reflects What the Mind Projects

If you have a low level of perception—that is, if you base your perceptions on only the physical, third-dimensional world—you will miss opportunities and remain stuck where you are. It's as simple as that. With a low level of perception, you are also susceptible to all the impurities and negativities of the material world that can drag you down. If you don't believe in the idea of projecting your future, you clearly aren't accessing the powers of the higher mind that exist within you, and you are resigning yourself to what is essentially a life of limitations. Unfortunately, so many people live their lives in a perpetual state of frustration and disappointment. This world is meant to be paradise, and sadly, it seems more like hell for a lot of people.

Much of our work here on earth is about getting in touch with that paradise within. What you put into the world with your vision is what you will get out of it. That's the basis of projection. A projection is sending out an image or thought from your mind into reality. When you look inward and project a positive future, you can prevent much of the negativity that currently exists in your life. Your capacity for happiness in your life is directly related to your powers of perception and your ability to project.

Your Powers of Perception

Everyone is equipped with the power of perception, but your ability to use it to positive ends depends on your willingness to be open. If you are skeptical, blocked, and consistently negative, and if you prefer to live in darkness instead of light, your life will reflect that, and you will be perpetually frustrated.

Bad experiences create destructive habits and negative thought patterns. We expect bad experiences, and they happen, which reinforces our beliefs. But if you open your mind, broaden your perception, and say, "Hey, I can turn my life around; I can live the life I want; I can project a new life for myself; I can manifest the life of my dreams," then you will do all that.

I have projected everything I've done in my life, whether it was becoming a famous singer, meeting my husband, or moving to America. I may have been afraid, I may have faced many obstacles and setbacks, but I have always created what I wanted. I always know that if I stick to my plan and have a strong vision, it will eventually happen.

When I finished writing my first book, my publisher told me that I needed a great endorsement from a well-known author. I had several endorsements from various clients, but none of them were best-selling authors. I began to concentrate on this because I knew it was up to me to make it happen.

One day, I was walking down the street, thinking about whom I could find and how I would find him or her, when a catalog caught my eye. A picture of Deepak Chopra was on the cover. I realized then that he was the person I needed to get to read and endorse my book. At the time, I had no way of reaching him directly, so I began to focus my attention on him in my mind. Even though he lived on the West Coast and didn't know me, I concentrated on having him read my book, and I even pictured his quote on its cover.

Two weeks later, my friend Jennifer invited me to a party. She sat me down next to a man I had never met before, and we started talking. After I shared with him some of my thoughts about the world, he said to me, "That's exactly the way Deepak Chopra talks about the world." He continued, "I'm Ray Chambers. I bring up Deepak's name only because he's my best friend." I told him about my book, and he said, "I'm meeting Deepak tomorrow. Why don't you come with me? He'd love to hear some of your ideas."

We met the next day, and Deepak said to me, "You needed me, and now I'm here because you made it happen. This is the way the mind works. I do the same thing all the time." He read the book and gave me the endorsement I needed.

The same law of attraction applies for everyone. Whether it's getting a new job, buying a house, or starting a new relationship—you name it—it can happen. It's all about being open to possibilities and setting clear intentions.

Putting Projections into Action

Laura

Whenever I talk about positive projection, one of the stories I love to tell is about my client Laura. Laura lived in

New York City but had always dreamed of having a house in the country for the weekends. In her mind she had a clear picture of her dream house, with a white fence and a front porch to read on. Laura didn't have a lot of money, and she knew that all the areas close to New York City were way beyond her finances. Nonetheless, she kept this vision of her house in the back of her mind.

One weekend she and her husband, John, were invited to a friend's wedding in a rural area they had never heard of that was about two hours outside the city. The reception was held on a farm owned by John's friend. And as soon as they arrived, Laura immediately fell in love with the beautiful surroundings. For the next year, she kept saying to John, "We have to find a farm like this. There must be something similar in the area that we can afford." She also began to put away a little bit of money every weekend.

About a year later, John got a phone call from his friend, inviting them to the farm for a visit. When they got there, their friends took them for a walk to show them the rest of their property. About a mile down the road, they turned a bend, and there Laura saw an old, white iron fence surrounding a farmhouse. As they approached, she saw it had a beautiful front porch. Laura gasped, "That's exactly the kind of house I've been dreaming about! You don't see old houses like that anymore, still unspoiled like this one." Then their friend told them that he had purchased the house for the surrounding property and was thinking about putting it on the market someday. Laura and John asked how much he wanted for it, and they were amazed that it was something they could afford. They made him an offer and worked out the details of the deal. Now Laura spends her weekends at her old farmhouse, sitting on her front porch, reading, and enjoying the view.

Lisa

Lisa wanted to know why she was still alone. She first came to me during the spring of 2001. "I'm forty-one; I've never been married," she told me. "What do you see in my future?"

When I told her I saw her having a child, a son, she was surprised. She said that after years of longing for a child, her time was running out, and she wasn't even in a committed relationship. She wanted to know how she could possibly have a son at this late date in her life. I told her she would be pregnant within a year and that the father of this child would come very soon.

At first Lisa scoffed; this sounded too good to be true. Nevertheless, she chose to work toward making my prediction come true. She decided to try in vitro fertilization. By the spring of 2002 she was pregnant, and she gave birth to a beautiful boy.

I then predicted that Lisa would marry the father of her son, a dear friend she had ventured into parenthood with because he had always wanted to be a father. Though neither of them expected it, they soon realized that their needs and desires were a perfect match, and they ended up getting married.

Lisa was able to break through her doubt and limiting beliefs about herself and change her way of thinking to project the future she desired. It took willingness, awareness, emotional effort, and commitment.

How We Attract Certain Events

The mind attracts and manifests events and develops patterns that are the result of old beliefs and conditioning. Attraction is based on the law of resonance: like attracts like. What you focus on will expand. That's how Laura manifested her dream. In the same way, replaying a past hurt or failure and focusing on disappointment simply reinforces those old messages and attracts more of the same back into your life.

We can also sabotage ourselves with negative emotions such as jealousy, anger, and fear. These feelings prevent us from making the good decisions we need to make and from taking actions we need to take. When you dwell on anger or jealousy, you send out negative energy that affects the people around you. When you are angry, you judge the world and even God. You cause disease in your body, and you are drawn to angry, jealous, and fearful people.

So often I meet single people who have been hurt by someone they loved deeply and cannot let go of their anger, sadness, or fear. They say, "I will never get married. There's no one out there for me." They believe it; by saying it, they project it, so they never do find love again. Harboring negative emotions and destructive thoughts can truly destroy our chances for receiving what is rightfully ours: a life of fulfillment and joy.

Agnes is a beautiful woman, born 5/9/1962, making her a 5. Her mother was angry and jealous of her all her life. At eighteen, Agnes ran away and married a man whom she divorced a year later. She has lived alone ever since, believing that she will never be with anyone.

Because she does not use her free will to manifest a relationship and believes she will never find one, Agnes will remain alone. As a double 5 (5 is her primary soul code as well as her birth month), she has difficulty attracting and attaching to someone. Psychologically, her mother created negative feelings of insecurity, fear, loneliness, and hopelessness in Agnes. When strong, negative feelings are aroused in Agnes and acted out in a destructive manner, she attracts negativity. These feelings can be traced to the memory of the original wound—in this case, her troubled relationship with her mother—and her bad marriage as a teenager.

If Agnes can process her negative emotions and heal them, instead of acting them out, she can create a strong bond of love and safety with a partner, despite the difficulties inherent in her code. For her, however, it will be a difficult struggle, because her code does not indicate ease in a love relationship.

You have the power to change these patterns, to stop attracting destructive relationships, and to start attracting helpful people, love, and success. We are all living in the here and now because we asked for an opportunity to heal our karma. Affirmations are a powerful way of healing this old information. We can let go of judgments we hold against ourselves and others by asking that they be replaced with love. We can also choose to surround ourselves with people who support us and love us unconditionally.

When Accidents Happen

We all know people who are always getting into accidents of some kind. If you are accident-prone, you need to examine whether or not you are blocked mentally, emotionally, or spiritually. You can also change the patterns you are stuck in so that you can avoid accidents and achieve your goals.

Accidents are often not accidents but the Universe's way of getting our attention. This was the case with Cameron, a young man from Southern California. The accident that nearly took his life actually ended up saving his life and the lives of many others.

Cameron was leading the California surfer's life, using construction work as a means of supporting his love of the ocean. But by the time he reached his early twenties, his passion for surfing was replaced by a passion for drugs and alcohol. One night about sixteen years ago, Cameron, in a drug-induced rage, ran into a busy street and was struck by a car. The accident was horrific. Cameron was badly hurt and barely hanging on to life. The Universe now had his full and undivided attention.

Cameron recovered in many ways. He made remarkable progress learning to walk and talk again. Drugs and alcohol were a thing of the past. Using physical therapy and the Feldenkrais Method, he regained partial mobility. His speech became intelligible. In meditation, Cameron found a peace that no drugs could ever provide, and he eventually became a practicing Buddhist. Over the next fifteen years, his remarkable spirit drove him to excel. He returned to school and got a master's degree in psychology. He dedicated himself to counseling others with drug and alcohol problems. Because of his history, which he freely shares, he has helped countless others break their addictions.

Cameron's goal is to surf again, which is why he called me. I told Cameron that it was possible and that he should talk with Jon Sweeney to continue healing his damaged arms and legs. At first, progress was slow, but he eventually regained strength and mobility in his arms and legs. After just months of therapy, the disfiguring scars on his right arm began to fade.

The breakthrough came when Cameron consulted me again and I told him he would soon regain his balance. Following my cue, Jon stopped working on individual body parts and started integrating Cameron's *chi* into a natural, balanced flow. It worked. As of this writing, Cameron has regained his balance and is able to walk and run without falling and has almost full use of his right arm. He is preparing to surf again, and I believe he will be on a surfboard within a matter of months. More importantly, he believes he will.

Cameron's recovery is an inspiration that shows us what we are capable of when we focus the mind and will.

The reasons behind accidents and other unpleasant events and changes may seem unclear when they are happening. You may ask yourself, "Why am I getting divorced?" or "Why didn't I get a promotion?" or "Why is my daughter behaving this way?" Only with introspection can such events begin to make sense. There are reasons why certain things are happening or lacking in your life. Knowing what they are requires learning how to read the signs so you can read and understand the higher purpose or lessons behind them.

Why Certain People Are Present in Our Lives

There is a strong relationship between your karma and what you accomplish in the future. Unresolved karmic issues keep you from moving forward. I have seen many cases of depression and addictive, compulsive, and suicidal behavior due to karmic pattern asking to be identified and healed. Karma can also explain why certain people appear in your life.

When Daniel called me for the first time I knew he was going through a lot of unresolved karma. Daniel is an 8, born 1/7/1962. He is a successful businessman, goal-oriented, attractive, and independent. As an 8, he loves children and wants a wife and family.

I saw he had a daughter but that she was not his. When I told him this, he was shocked and didn't know what to say. Then he told me that when he was twenty-one, he had had a one-night stand. Seven months later, the woman showed up at his door, seven months pregnant, and asked him to marry her. He knew he was not ready for such a commitment, and although he chose not to marry her, he agreed to pay child support and did so for thirteen years.

"I love this girl and have gotten used to the idea that I'm her father," he said.

At first Daniel didn't want to do a paternity test to prove I was right. When he did, he was devastated to learn that, indeed, the girl was not his. Nonetheless, he kept his agreement to love and care for the child. The session helped him understand that this was the way he had chosen to repay his karmic debts in this life. Now that he has made peace with his choice, he is happy and ready to marry.

When Free Will Interferes with Destiny

For Anna, it was part of her destiny that she worked at a major magazine with a famous journalist who was one of my clients. I didn't know Anna but felt her through the journalist when he came for a reading one day. I told him there was a woman he worked with who was sick and had a tumor. He agreed to send her to me.

Anna came with her husband. I told her that she had a tumor in her brain and that it was inoperable. I also told her that it would shrink and disappear with the right therapy; once again, I recommended Jon Sweeney.

A doctor confirmed her tumor, and Anna began to work with Jon on a regular basis. Several months later the tumor was gone. She sent me an e-mail and told me that I had saved her life. Then she told me that she would be undergoing chemotherapy treatment. I was alarmed and begged her not to.

She chose not to listen. I later learned that she had died from a treatment overdose. Was it meant to be? Absolutely not! But she chose to override her destiny.

When Destiny Interferes with Free Will

Sometimes our will is no match for our destiny.

When my father was young, he attended law school, but he was not happy with the laws in Romania and didn't want to be a communist. After he graduated, he served in World War II, and when the war ended he decided to change his career. He earned a degree in economics and become a manager at a local bank.

One day the bank informed him that he would be transferred to a bank in another town. He was upset and told them he didn't want to go, but they made his life so miserable that he knew he had to leave. Several months after he had moved, he saw a woman at a bus station. Mesmerized by her beauty, he followed her. To his surprise, he discovered that she worked in the same bank. That woman became his wife—and my mother!

Despite my father's strong will and resistance to change, it was his destiny to meet my mother and give birth to me. Because my father surrendered to his destiny, his path brought him much happiness and success.

When to Act, When to Surrender

When destiny interferes with free will, it's important to recognize the point at which we need to surrender. This is usually when there is a larger plan at work; at the time, we can see only one portion of it. In my father's case, the Universe made it clear that if he did not surrender to his destiny, he would continually encounter obstacles to happiness. The wise part of him listened and turned to where the road was open and clear—to a new life where he would meet his destiny.

When we've done all we can and taken all the steps we needed to complete a plan, yet obstacle after obstacle keeps us from seeing it through, that's often the Universe's way of telling us to step back and allow our path to be shown to us, even if it's through one step at a time. Sometimes an illness or accident can be the Universe's message for surrender.

Overuse of the Will

The will is a powerful tool for manifesting, but we can also abuse it and get carried away with our desire for control. When we overuse our will, we not only seek to excessively control our own destiny but also to control the destiny of others. This abuse of will happens when the will is aligned with the ego, or the lower self.

We assume we know what's good for others, not based on precognition but on our ego's needs and desires. In truth, we have no way of knowing what is in the highest good of another or how others will choose to fulfill their agreements in this life. While others' choices may be painful to observe, interfering in people's destiny without their consent is taking away their soul's journey.

We all know people who walk into a room and immediately want to take control of a situation and everyone's part in it. They have difficulty listening and receiving from others but are always giving information or advice. Caretakers often suffer from abuse of the will. One example is that of parents who excessively control their children and household. While their intentions may appear to be good, they assume they know best and impose their will without truly considering the needs of others in the moment. While providing children with boundaries is appropriate for their well-being, excessive caretaking denies them their ability to exercise free will and to learn from their own mistakes and experiences.

People with overactive wills also harm themselves. They assert the desire of their ego over the needs of their soul and interfere with their own highest good. Even when they make the effort to seek help from a therapist or psychic, they already "know" what's best for them and are not open to what comes through in the session. Often people come to me for advice and then don't take it. That was the unfortunate case with Margit.

I worked with Margit and her husband, Roger, many years ago. They were beautiful people who looked great together, but they held very different beliefs. He was spiritual and happy by nature, while she was interested in acquiring wealth and success in the material world. She sold expensive jewelry at Bergdorf Goodman and made a good income, but that was not enough. Her goal was to be rich.

"I work with rich people and I want to be like them, have a big house, and afford that lifestyle," she said to me.

One day she came to me alone and told me that she felt she was not rich because of Roger. She felt that he was not making money and she wanted to divorce him. My advice to her was not to do it. If she did, I predicted that she would regret it later. She put her free will to use, ignored my advice, and divorced him. He was devastated.

Three years later, Margit was married to a wealthy man from Bergdorf. Meanwhile, Roger had become involved with a woman from Italy who was sweet and spiritual like him. They decided to move in together and found a beautiful house.

The next time I heard from Roger, he told me that Margit was calling him all the time and wanting to see him. I told him to invite her into his home and introduce her to his future wife. For Margit it was a disaster. She became so jealous and angry that she couldn't stand to be in the house and quickly left.

For Roger, the incident was reassuring. By staying true to himself, he found his happiness and peace. He and his beloved got married in Italy. Margit, on the other hand, used her free will to choose to ignore her spiritual development and chase after material wealth. Even though she is now a billionaire, she calls Roger to complain about her jealousy, grief, and unhappiness. She has lost love—the true abundance.

Behind the need to gain power and control through our ego is fear, the opposite of love. Fear of losing control, fear of being exposed, fear of being "naked" in the eyes of God, fear of intimacy—all come down to our fear of surrendering the ego. But surrendering the needs of our ego to feed our soul is a primary part of our work. It's how we make room for more goodness and more God.

8

The Importance of Responsibility: Working for the Good

You have the ability to turn your life around, from negative to positive, and to create beauty and fulfillment in your life. The powers within you are to be used to create good. They should never be used irresponsibly—to cause harm or damage—no matter how badly someone has hurt or betrayed you. You will get back what you put out in life. If you put harm out into the world, you will be the one who is harmed.

One of the best reasons for working on yourself is that by doing so, you have a positive effect not only on your own life but on the lives of everyone you know and even on the world around you. You can tell you're on the right path when you start to feel more at peace with yourself, even if things have not changed that much outwardly, as with Gabriella, who wrote:

"I have deepened my connection with the Holy Spirit so much during this last month. I have never felt happier and more at peace. It is illogical to a part of my mind since I am still single, I have not heard from Tim, I am moving into my house before the construction is complete, and I still have the same job. Yet I have never been happier and more at peace. I feel a lot—I mean a lot—of internal changes happening with me lately, so my higher self tells me this feeling is not illogical at all.

"This is truly an entirely different way in which I am starting to live, and it feels uncomfortable at times, but it feels very good the rest of the time. I have discovered that I need to focus on one day at a time, and as long as I am focused and centered on Spirit, then everything else will fall into place. Thank you again for keeping me on the right path for myself."

When a note on a musical instrument is sounded, the same note on a nearby instrument also vibrates. That's the law of resonance. When the two single sound waves are in harmony, they merge and become one wave, and the sound we hear is amplified. The same goes for our vibration and what we put out in the world. What we feel inside is what we are adding to the world.

Aligning with Destiny

There is so much good you can accomplish in your own life. If you align with your destiny and use your free will to amplify your purpose in the world, you'll find you will have a natural desire to share yourself in the world for the greater good. Whether it's volunteering for a cause you care about, teaching others a skill you excel at, or extending kindness to strangers, aligning with your destiny lets you break out of self-centeredness and see the needs of those around you.

When you work for the good, you stop being selfish because you work from your heart. You integrate your life and the way you serve the world, and your path becomes guided and synchronous. Overall, we are missing the boat on service, though that tide is clearly changing. Doing service for others breaks us out of our small world and unifies us as a human family.

If we each choose to bring goodness, peace, and abundance into our lives, then by the law of resonance it will spread beyond us. It's simple: For every affirmation you think or speak and for every goal you seek to achieve, add the words, "for the greatest good of all."

The Universal Laws

In *Everyday Karma*, I discussed in detail the importance of the Universal Laws and how they can help us attain perfection and connect to the Universal Intelligence. Operating outside these laws causes suffering and imbalance; working within these laws will help you create a life in harmony with the Universe and your soul purpose.

Here is a brief review:

* *The Law of Karma* (the most important law). Every thought, word, deed, and feeling creates karma that you must resolve.

* *The Law of Wisdom*. Acknowledge what you have the power to change and what you don't.

* *The Law of Evolution*. The way to wisdom is through spiritual evolution.

* *The Law of Vibrational Energy*. Nothing is fixed; everything is transforming.

* *The Law of Oneness*. We are all one.

* *The Law of Love*. We are here to love; love is the answer to everything.

* *The Law of Abundance*. The Universe provides us with limitless abundance.

✳ *The Law of Divine Order.* Trust that there is a divine plan at work in the Universe.

✳ *The Law of Gratitude.* Take nothing for granted and be grateful for everything.

✳ *The Law of Harmony.* Honor the perfection of the Universe.

✳ *The Law of Manifestation.* What you think, you call into being.

✳ *The Law of Detachment.* Reaching Dharma requires letting go of attachments.

✳ *The Law of Attitude.* How you treat yourself and others creates karma.

✳ *The Law of Acceptance.* What you resist, you become.

✳ *The Law of Duality.* The Universe is made of opposites—yin/yang, male/female, dark/light.

✳ *The Law of Trinity.* We are made of three elements—mind, body, and spirit—that must work in harmony.

✳ *The Law of Attraction.* What you are, you will attract.

✳ *The Law of Divinity.* We are here to realize our divinity.

✳ *The Law of Cycles.* There are stages through which we reach new awareness.

* *The Law of Destiny*. We are here to fulfill our destiny through experience.

* *The Law of Dharma*. We must align ourselves with the ultimate order of things and fulfill our mission.

If we want to reach peace and stability, we must pay attention to these laws and make them a part of our everyday lives. Our future is waiting.

PART III

Letting the Future In

9

The Art of Prediction:
Tapping the Seven Tools of the Mind

The art of prediction has a long history. For thousands of years people have been using various arts to foretell the future: astrology, numerology, the Kabala, the I Ching, the pendulum, oracles, and the vision quest. Divination tools continue to fascinate people and can be used effectively, but the tools of your own mind are just as powerful.

Thanks to modern science, we now know more about the mind's potential than ever before. Researchers have extensively studied the 90 percent of the brain that we don't use, and we are beginning to learn how to tap into its power. We all have this remarkable potential but have been afraid to use it.

Conscious Mind and Subconscious Mind

It's important to realize that when we are afraid,
we are not imagining the future. We are
reliving the distant past.

DIANA COOPER, *A Time for Transformation*

Before we can understand the difference between the conscious and subconscious mind, we have to understand how the brain works. Psychology has gained many insights through explorations of the neurosciences. But even with all the research, science is accepting the idea that when it comes to core brain activity, we are not all that different from animals; in fact, 90 percent of our brain activity is exactly the same as that of animals. We depend on the ganglion system—the neuron network of our autonomous nerves—to keep our internal organs working, especially when we sleep, as animals do. Moreover, part of our brain is reptilian, and this ancient part connects us with many of our negative emotions.

We have also learned much about the brain's energy field. Many researchers have sought to demonstrate that the brain generates electricity. Dr. Hans Berger, an Austrian neuropsychiatrist, was the first to prove the existence of the brain's electrical waves. He named them alpha and beta waves, and in the 1920s, he recorded the first electro-encephalograms (EEGs) in humans. He later demonstrated that all life manifests in the electrodynamic field. What this means is that life is the by-product of awareness, and the functions of the brain are associated with the electro-dynamic field.

. If we accept the fact that we're electrical gadgets, we realize that we function on two levels: the level of the conscious mind and the level of the subconscious, or the dream state. In the subconscious realm, dreams are a result of the impression left by memories. The dream state is similar to the process of our physical metabolism in that all the experiences which we haven't digested will appear in our dreams. When a sensory impulse enters the right hemisphere of the brain, the brain records an emotional impression. If an act, such as touching water or eating an apple, occurs in the physical dimension and creates a sensory impulse, the memory of that act goes into the brain and creates an emotional memory. All day long you accumulate sensory impressions that are stored in the cells of the right brain. While you're awake, your body reacts accordingly and prepares an action. Once you go to sleep, however, you have to digest all the experiences you haven't dealt with.

The Birth of Thought

We have all gone from a state of sleeping in our mother's womb to a state of waking when are born into the sensory world. From that moment, you bring with you all your memories plus all the abilities you are born with.

Our reptilian brain is where our emotions or emotional response can become very powerful, depending on the impulse we receive. All our sensory perceptions would have no meaning without a link to a memory. Based on how your mind responds to the sensory data, you create thoughts. All sensory input and impressions become associated with memories that already exist in the cortex, and a thought is born. What was subconscious becomes conscious.

In order for an impulse to become a thought, it must travel from the right brain and into the cerebral cortex, which is considered the seat of our intelligence. The cerebral cortex is where we understand, manufacture, interpret, and analyze. There is an old saying about counting to one hundred before you act on an impulse. That's about the time it takes for an impulse to reach the cortex. Waiting helps ensure that you understand what you're really doing before you do it.

Our dreams, then, are all those impressions that the mind needs to digest to maintain balance. That's why not getting enough sleep can wreak havoc with our mental health and physical well-being. When we sleep, our body manufactures a protein that is vital to sustaining our health. A sound sleep depends on several factors, but it mainly depends on the level of adrenaline in the bloodstream. It's that deep sleep which enables the brain to process all stored memories.

People who experience phobias, which I discussed in chapter 6, are dealing with emotions that have been repressed for a long time. Those emotions come from different stages of their lives or from prior lives. Until those impressions are consciously processed, they will keep popping up and wreaking havoc.

How can you tap into all your memories? You begin by getting to know the right side of the brain. Using tools such as hypnotherapy, meditation, and similar techniques that put the mind in an alpha state allows you to reconnect and recover the sensory impulses and more.

Right Brain versus Left Brain

When Einstein wrote the law of the gravity, he did so in a dream state. He said, "In order to complete the law of gravity, I have to sleep on the right side of my brain." He meant that while he slept, he was able to access his right brain—

the side that dreams and goes beyond linear time. Einstein understood the power of being able to tap into his right brain, which led him to his greatest discoveries.

The right hemisphere of the brain oversees many more activities than the left. The left brain controls your motor skills and language and all the skills necessary for your body's physical movement. So when you are walking, taking care of your daily work, and enjoying recreational activities, you're operating from the left brain, for the most part. The right hemisphere is the brain's creative sensory storehouse. It is most active when you enter a state of altered consciousness, like hypnosis.

The right side of the brain is where the infinite potential of the mind exists. If we ever tap into that extraordinary magnetic field, we will experience the possibility of employing the highly creative mind, seeing beyond the physical world, breaking through the sensory level of perception, and going beyond space and time. That's when the mind will see extraordinary things.

Tapping into the 90 Percent

Humanity is slowly headed in the direction of unlocking the unused 90 percent of the brain. The latest scientific research tells us we have already gone from using 3 percent of the brain two thousand years ago to using 10 percent today. All the energies influencing the electromagnetism of the brain and all the forces in the Universe will increase the speed at which the brain functions, allowing it to operate more and more at its natural potential.

At the very moment we begin to unlock that 90 percent, we are no longer trapped in the physical dimension. We will have the ability to be clairvoyant and clairaudient, to see and hear psychically. Every conflict that's manifested in the world—all the diseases, traumas, and problems—is a reflection of the fact that we are not using our inborn abilities to actually heal and that we don't fully understand how we function.

One example of the mind's potential is when it detaches from the body, such as in astral travel or when people go into a coma. Physically you're paralyzed and you don't sense anything; your connection with the sensory world is broken. But your brain is still functioning and understands everything. If you talk to people in a coma, they know exactly what you're telling them although they don't necessarily keep these recordings as accessible memories in their brains. Even though there's no response to the sensory stimuli, the brain continues to record and register everything.

According to ancient teachings, including Buddhism, Babylonian philosophy, and the Kabala, the physical body dies on three levels, leaving the three physical elements—earth, water, and fire. But the electrodynamic field of the brain continues to operate for at least another forty days. All the sacred teachings about the forty days after death—such as the forty days that passed after Jesus came back from the dead—reflect this phenomenon of the brain. Ancient civilizations, starting with Lemuria and ending with Buddhism, had instructions to not touch the body for forty days. Since the 1980s, scientists have been investigating the human electromagnetic field, and they're coming to the same conclusion. There are clearly many mysteries yet to be uncovered about how the brain functions.

To begin tapping into that mysterious 90 percent, you have to operate at the highest level of your perception. You can increase your vibration by engaging in activities such as meditation, deep relaxation, and self-hypnosis. If all your time is spent in the mundane world, going through your daily routine, it's likely that you're not tapping into the 90 percent or receiving messages from the other side. You have to make time to connect, to build the bridges to the Invisible World.

Intuition: Bridging the Left and Right Brain

By drawing on the information that is stored in the right side of the brain and tapping into your infinite potential, you begin to awaken dormant impressions and memories that you have carried for a long time, including those from the DNA in your genetic code.

When we make something conscious, the right brain sends a signal to the left brain. These signals come for a minute or a fraction of a second; they are visions, flashes of insight, channeled messages, or premonitions. In order for that connection to occur, however, the two parts of the brain must work together. Usually people who work with their brain, such as scientists, philosophers, doctors, and those in the arts, are tuned in to their creative and intuitive side and have a stronger bridge between the two hemispheres. Therefore they receive most of their impressions.

As with any muscle, the more you work the brain, the stronger it gets. The more brain potential you build, the greater your ability to become a seer and to act on your intuition. Intuition is actually the thread between the two sides of the brain.

Two major glands are responsible for this thread connecting the left and right hemispheres: the pineal gland and the pituitary gland. These glands carry the signal from the highest intuitive level to the lower level of thought. Generally speaking, the conscious mind is considered the lower level of consciousness, because it deals with the world of density and matter.

We all live on these two levels every day. As we go through our daily routine, we usually operate on the lower level, relying more on the reptilian brain and our emotions to guide us through our day. Then when we go to sleep, we drop the reptilian brain. In the dream state, we don't need our emotions or our conscious mind. Instead, we enter the higher level of seeing.

By exploring the mind, you flex your muscles of awareness; you learn how to work with consciousness to tap the subconscious mind and all its gifts and to begin to make use of all the highly imaginative, creative skills with which you were born.

Within each of us lies this amazing potential. The more you detach from the material world and explore the depths of your being, the more you discover these unexplored territories within and open the doorways to your authentic power.

The fear of seeing has blocked us for the past two thousand years. We feel we don't have a right to this autonomous power; we think it is hubris. Instead of relying on ourselves, we've relied on faith in the world's

religions to guide us. But all we have to do to guide ourselves is to make use of what we are born with—the Seven
Tools of the Mind:

* *Intelligence*. The faculty of reasoning, knowing, and
  thinking. All the capabilities of the brain are there for
  us to utilize to acquire the knowledge and information
  we need.

* *Imagination*. The mental faculty of forming images or
  concepts of external objects not present in cognitive
  reality. Imagination is more powerful than knowledge
  because it is the doorway to the higher mind and other
  dimensions.

* *Intuition*. The perception of the reality beyond cognitive
  reality and linear time. Intuition forms the bridge to the
  subconscious mind. In order to use your intuition, your
  subconscious has to be clear.

* *Logic*. The principles of reasoning, based on the physical world of the senses: smell, taste, and touch. Logic
  enables us to make sense of our physical world.

* *Creativity*. The expression of the imagination. Creativity
  is our manifesting tool. Our creative faculty allows us to
  visualize what we want to bring into being.

* *Memory.* The mental faculty by which events are recalled. Events are stored in the subconscious mind, and they create your karma.

* *Energy.* The power through which the mind vibrates; the force of thinking as well as the force of all emotions and feelings.

Each of us possesses all seven of these tools, but most of us tend to rely on just a few of them—usually the ones we feel most comfortable with. Some of us use a lot of creativity and imagination but don't balance it with logic. Or we may use our intelligence and memory but not enough of our intuition.

The key to creating our own future reality and living a fully empowered life is having a fully empowered mind. The art of prediction happens when you use all the tools of the mind in equal measure.

10

Developing Your Visionary Skills: If You Can See It, You Can Achieve It

Manifesting your goals requires a combination of vision, intention, awareness, acknowledgment, and action. First, you must have vision and know what it is you want. Second, you must acknowledge where you are in your life, what cycle of life you are in, and your circumstances. Then you can make it happen.

Manifesting your goals is an amazing mental process. In truth, your goal is already part of your subconscious mind; your mission has already been implanted. You might be destined to be a singer, but if you never try to sing, never practice, or have no idea that this is your destiny, it cannot happen. Your work is to bring it into consciousness through action.

The Chemistry of Thinking

Perception and thought are crucial to creating your reality, and the power of thoughts and words actually works on the level of our cells and DNA. To understand how to develop your ability to see your future, it's helpful to understand how the brain functions on the cellular level.

When neuroscientists studied the brain in recent years to understand how it works, they found that it contains 11 billion neurons. These neurons are composed of millions of molecules of ribonucleic acid (RNA), which makes up our DNA. They also determined that the highest functions of the brain are achieved by the way in which the neurons alter the protein they form. The brain's ability to function is based on this interaction between these nerve cells and the brain protein. In simple terms, the sensory data or charge is picked up by the neuron, which alters the brain protein, similar to the way a computer circuit picks up data and deposits it in the computer memory by changing the arrangement of its codes. Every protein, then, is a chemical representation of thoughts. Neurons show us scientifically that there is a definite connection between the world of matter and the world of spirit!

It's quite amazing when you consider that these 11 billion neurons perform so many billions of activities necessary for our existence. Science has also determined that many telepathic actions occur in the brain. When we concentrate and create thoughts, the brain sends out many mental messages to other people and into the world around us. This phenomenon is called telepathy. Telepathy is not an unusual gift that only a few people are capable of; it's a natural ability of the brain that we are all born with.

We know that the brain is the central processor of our thoughts, feelings, personality, and behavior. When people are overcome by many obstacles in their life, such as excessive fear, negative emotions, and adversity, the question is, how can they work with the brain to break this chain of abnormal behavior?

Changing Behavior

When you study psychology, you will soon learn about abnormal behaviors. The list is long: learning disorders; psychotic disorder; paranoia; mood disorders; bipolar disorders; anxiety; panic attacks; specific phobias and social phobias; obsessive and compulsive behavior; post-traumatic stress disorder; pain disorders (when you think you have pain but can't locate it); disassociation (being in denial about who you are); eating disorders; and personality disorders. These problems are clear signs that a person is dealing with a serious inner conflict. Such disorders are the source of great suffering for many people. They interfere with normal brain function and keep people from functioning and living normal lives.

Until we heal such imbalances, it's nearly impossible to develop the abilities of our higher mind in a responsible and beneficial way. It's our responsibility as individuals to work on ourselves and make sure we take the time to heal any abnormal behaviors that are blocking our natural creative intelligence. The question, then, is where to begin. How do you resolve these self-conflicts and reclaim your ability to function and move forward?

First you need to identify the source of your problem; you need to discover the belief or thought that is generating the abnormal behavior. As a therapist, I use two different approaches or techniques from traditional psychology that can help determine the source of these disorders so that you can be free of them.

Cognitive Therapy

Cognitive therapy works with the conscious mind to help change thoughts and patterns of thinking. When you enter this type of therapy, you acknowledge your destructive thinking and behavior. You are aware that you are unhappy and that you want to change your patterns of negative thinking into positive, constructive ones. You affirm that you want to fully participate in your life and to be vital and at peace with yourself.

In this work you draw upon all the skills of the conscious mind, combined with the infinite abilities of the brain to heal itself. You resource its intelligence, energy, and memory as well as the seven tools of the mind outlined in the previous chapter, which we are blessed with at birth.

The best psychologists are the ones who operate on the cognitive level rather than on the subconscious, because they wake people up and bring the person back to the real world. The cognitive approach shows how you impact your life directly when you change the thoughts that influence how you interact with the world.

Psychodynamic Therapy

Another therapeutic approach is the psychodynamic approach, or psychoanalysis. In psychoanalysis, you work with your unconscious feelings and bring them into conscious awareness. In this form of therapy, you are able to tap into the unconscious and find the source of the conflict: the original event or trauma that has been repressed. By bringing the unconscious feelings to the surface, you can release the emotional memory and clear what was triggering the abnormal or compulsive behavior or thought. When this level of self-conflict goes unchecked, it can develop into a manic-depressive state and create a bipolar disorder. If you're in a conflict with your environment, you can go into an anxiety disorder or panic disorder.

Overcoming Fears, Obstacles, and Adversities

Both psychoanalysis and cognitive therapy can help identify the source of the problem that is creating obsessive and destructive behavior in your life. Using these two therapy techniques, you can change your life by changing your attitude and perception of yourself. When you address and heal these core issues, you are also changing the nature of the energy that you generate—the telepathic signals that you are sending out into the world. We know that like attracts like, so generating new energy changes what you attract into your life. Once you are free of the past, you have the clarity and energy to develop and use all the abilities of your brain.

Testing Yourself

There are also activities you can do to test your brain. In school we often don't like the idea of tests, and we may experience anxieties over exams. But tests are simply tools to measure where you are on a cognitive level. They can also give you an opportunity to exercise your mental and cognitive skills. IQ or intelligence tests, for example, can test your verbal reasoning, visual skills, and memory. It may also surprise you to see where your strengths and weaknesses are. When you look at the results, do so without any judgment. See them simply as useful information that can show you if there is an area you would like to improve.

Distinguishing between Fact and Illusion

Because of all the billions of neurons, the more you tap into the mind, the easier it is to go from fact to illusion very quickly. To distinguish between the two you must be vigilant in paying attention and centering yourself. Use all the tools of the mind to remain clear. Say to yourself, "This is the part of my life that is fact; I can comprehend where I can take action in the world of matter" and "This is the part where I am living in an illusion."

When we are not paying attention, the mind can fall asleep. That's why tools are useful; they help us exercise our abilities and stay focused. The mind has to be brought back to nature, to hear sounds, and to play in the physical dimensions. These steps keep us from getting lost in the illusions of thoughts run amuck.

Developing the Abilities of the Brain

There are several activities you can do to empower your brain, enhance your awareness, and make the most of the Seven Tools of the Mind. Take these activities at your own pace. For example, try focusing on one suggestion in the first week. When you feel that it has become a natural part of your routine and you feel some positive effects, move on to the next suggestion. To track your progress, you can note any changes or impressions in a journal.

1. Work with nature, the environment, and the beauty of the world around you. Nature nurtures. Whether it's swimming in the ocean, planting and tending a garden, or simply taking a walk, spending time in the natural world reconnects you with the natural patterns and cycles of the Universe. It helps to reset your natural clock, and it is a pleasurable and powerful way to heighten your sensibilities and develop your intuition.

2. Express issues that relate to the meaning of life. People who become more spiritual contemplate these deeper issues, which are the provenance of the soul. Many wonderful, thought-provoking books are available to us to stimulate deeper thinking. The more you explore and

investigate life's meaning and why you are here, the more you open and develop that part of the brain which relates to the psychic mind.

3. Express your needs, moods, and authentic feelings. Stay tuned in to your own destiny by truthfully saying what you feel and noticing your dominant emotions. Teach yourself to stay with the brighter side of feelings, such as love, compassion, and acceptance. By expressing yourself truthfully and not denying what you feel toward yourself and others, you will naturally lighten up and find that your mood swings will dissipate as you become more in harmony with yourself and your surroundings.

4. Use the power of sound, language, and music to create harmony in your life. Sound has been used for centuries as a healing tool in ayurvedic and other teachings. *Harmony* means "free of harm." Pay attention to words, what you say, and how you say it. Be mindful of the words you use to describe yourself and others. Explore sound therapy, toning, and music. Sound waves are a potent way to tap into the higher mind and balance yourself energetically.

5. Express yourself physically. Explore mind/body therapies such as dancing and yoga. Using the body's abilities in exercise and play not only improves our physical health, but it also enhances our natural mind/body balance.

6. Use suggestion and motivation. Suggestion and motivation therapies such as hypnotherapy and visualization are effective tools for healing problems based on inner conflict and wounds in the subconscious. Suggestion and motivation direct the behavior and lead to goal-oriented behavior. Goal-setting is a critical part of creating your future. There is a direct connection between your behavior and your goals, since what you think and feel affects the way you express yourself and your future possibilities. When you have goal-oriented behavior, you use your maximum intelligence and make the most of your personality and gifts.

7. Use the energy and healing power of the brain. We can heal everything in the physical body through the power of the mind. See the mind as your most powerful healing tool and begin working with your intentions and affirmations to tap into and direct its healing energy.

These keys will help you develop all the tools of the mind. By empowering the mind, you will begin to truly acknowledge and accept who you are, and from that powerful point you will have the ability to see and project what is in store for you.

Using the Brain's Healing Energy

Your thoughts emanate a specific vibration, and that vibration exits the body through the fingers. This vibration is powerful enough to get into the bloodstream, and this flow of energy is what makes up your bioenergetic field, or auric field. Your auric field is directly connected to your thinking; therefore, you vibrate out what you think through your fingers into the world around you.

Sometimes you may notice that when you sit near people, you can feel their vibration. We say that someone has a "good vibe" or "bad vibe." Whether or not they say a word, you can sense what they are emanating.

Extraordinary teachers throughout the ages healed others with their hands. Jesus healed people with his hands, but it was through a process generated by his mind. His mind generated specific vibrations that traveled through the hands. When he touched people's auric field, he made miracles happen. This is the basis for the many subtle energy healing practices, such as Reiki and Polarity therapies.

The mind can also be engaged to heal the body by healing the belief system. Your beliefs are part of your programming. In a state of deep relaxation, you can use guided imagery or visualization to journey inside the body and visit where the illness or block is. Ask the body what belief you are holding is behind this illness or disease, and then listen for the answer. Once you know the reason and are willing to change it or let it go, you remove the patterning that helped create the disease. Then your healing process can begin.

When the mind is stuck, it is empowering to work against what's holding you back, and it is exciting to know that you really can overcome the obstacles you face. When you use the infinite potential of the brain, you can achieve absolutely everything; your future becomes your creation.

By putting all these tools together, you create and build a new awareness of Self. From there it's just a matter of visualizing: What do I want to set in motion? What do I want to create? How do I see my future self? Where and with whom?

At that point, you will see that your future becomes something which is easy to comprehend. It stops seeming abstract, scary, parapsychological, or occult. The future becomes reality, set in motion by proper use of the mind in all its power.

All your life experiences are your own creation. You have to use your reason to create them, and they, in turn, will reveal the true nature of yourself. Acquiring self-knowledge is a significant way to discover why you are here and the many goals you can accomplish. Freud and Einstein said that everything is in your mind. If you shift your thinking, you shift the world.

If humanity shifts its thinking, we can shift the world from the way it is today; we can go from suffering and conflict to paradise. We can operate beyond time, and everything can change—in a multidimensional minute.

11

Manifesting Your Reality:
Seven Steps to Master Your Future

Descartes said, "I think, therefore I am." Take that idea one step further: "What you think, you become." As you have seen, your world is ruled by your mind and the thoughts it creates. Your thinking produces your states of consciousness, and your consciousness creates your physical reality.

It is so important to be conscious of your thought patterns. If you are unhappy with your physical reality, you can change it by changing the way you think and manifest a new reality.

You can read your own mind in so far as you can read and understand your needs, weaknesses, strengths, dreams, and desires. Once you have this self-awareness, you can create new goals. Your dream world and your logical world are interconnected, but you must pay attention to what is happening between the two realities so you can put them in sync. We all have life events we need to go through, and from them we learn lessons that can help us project the future.

We are the only ones who are capable of reading ourselves at this level. No one else can do it for us. This is not God's work; it is our work, and we must take the steps required to create the life and the future we want.

How to Employ Your Will Constructively to Master Your Destiny

Power is willpower. Learning how to create your future is about effective use of your will. When you employ your willpower for a constructive purpose, you become the master of your destiny. The road to self-mastery begins simply: by replacing destructive, compulsive, and non-engaging behavior and thoughts with constructive patterns and actions. Here are steps to take to fully employ your will. Think about your destiny and use these steps to help shape the path that will lead you to its fulfillment. You may find it useful to concentrate on one step at a time. As you explore each step and make a permanent place for it in your own life, you can turn your focus to the next one when you are ready.

1. Concentrate on a single purpose in life, and be sure that this purpose is right for you.

2. Choose a task. In order to successfully accomplish your goals, you must choose a task and see it through. Make sure this task is a constructive one. We have a tendency to engage in destructive and compulsive behaviors rather than constructive ones, so choosing a task in life requires a conscious choice.

3. Refuse failure. Never accept the idea that you will fail at something; believe that you will succeed.

4. Use the force of your will to accomplish your goal, and know it's within your power to achieve it.

5. Always keep your mind centered on your purpose.

6. Have no fear in life, because fear exhausts life's energy. Fear is the greatest enemy of willpower.

7. Even if you "fail," see failure as the best opportunity for sowing success.

8. Use self-analysis in a positive way. Avoid self-judgment and criticism.

9. Realize the creative power of initiative; the power of your initiative will lead to your success. We always create something from nothing through the inventive power of our spirit.

10. Learn to see the good in everyone. This will enable you to rise above the weakness of the ego.

11. Free yourself from bad habits and addictions; they impede your growth.

12. Success is measured by happiness and by your state of mind.

The Keys to Success

Success is not measured by material wealth, power, or money. It's the ability to remain in harmony with the Universal Laws. If you possess happiness, then you possess everything. From my own life and from listening to the experiences of my clients, I have learned many truths about success:

* Success does not depend on your training, or your abilities, or your luck but rather on your determination to make use of the opportunities that are presented to you.

* Opportunities don't come by chance—we create them. Some opportunities are implanted in your DNA at birth, but how and when they develop depends on you. You have the choice to take what you have been given and turn it into a masterpiece. Using our gifts to our best advantage is the lesson of life.

✳ Most of the time, we use our natural abilities to develop the powers that God gave us—our divine gifts. Our willpower and the power of thought are also divine gifts. Our responsibility in using these gifts is only ours.

✳ Set positive intentions. Because the mind is constantly battling negativity, one positive thought is not enough to attract success. We need to change our habitual thinking and shift our negativity into many positive thoughts. We hear a lot about positive thinking, but unfortunately, at the subconscious level we often project the dark instead of the light. With positive intentions, you always find the light, even in dark times.

✳ Surrender your problems. When you want to correct a problem, don't review it over and over again. Instead, let it rest; let it sink deep into the dark region of your inner self. Let it integrate into the self, without judgment, and attune with your soul. With surrender, you will be able to realign your thoughts with your actions. Then you will feel the shift and see the turning point within yourself.

✳ Aim high. Conscious will is the vital force, accompanied by determination and effort. Use your power to do things you thought you couldn't do. The more you build your confidence in your own abilities, the higher you will aim. Again, the Invisible Mind is the creator of everything. When you employ your mind for constructive purposes, you become the master of your own destiny.

You are now equipped with the keys to see your own destiny for yourself and create the life you've always wanted. I hope you use these tools to your full advantage to realize all the potential you have within. To aid you in this empowering journey of discovery, here is a summary of the principles discussed in the previous chapters. You can return to this summary from time to time for direction, guidance, and encouragement.

Seven Steps to Master Your Future

1. *Acknowledge your soul code and the cycle you are currently in.* Then acknowledge that you have the power to create change and make a better future. You are not stuck. Become an honest observer of your own life. Focus your attention on where you are and what you have right now. Think about what is working and what isn't. Eliminate any negative thoughts of hopelessness, and realize you can create the life or specific goals you want.

2. *Accept everything that has happened to you.* Do this without victimizing yourself, blaming yourself, or feel-

ing regret. Look at where you are in your life from a fresh, objective perspective, and ask yourself what lessons you have learned or could still learn from these events. You cannot change the past, but you can change your perception of it.

3. *Let go of blockages, resistance, and feelings of negativity.* Take a look at each problem you are facing individually and project them out of linear time, one by one.

4. *Analyze and observe your thoughts.* Review every mental message your mind is giving you during different events and circumstances. Are there negative thoughts that are preventing you from moving forward? Are you carrying around a faulty or obsolete belief system?

5. *Create a vision and project it outward.* Once you know what you want to manifest, create a clear and detailed image of it in your mind's eye, and hold it there. This step involves using your imagination. By engaging your imagination, you break linear time with the power of your mind. Everything you put there will transform and manifest. Your future exists within you.

6. *Manifest your vision into reality.* Make a plan and stick to it. What needs to change and what needs to be eliminated or added to make your vision a reality? This step requires your logical mind, your energy, and your ability to act. Working from the point of view that your vision is possible, what can you do to move things

along? After you have taken the appropriate actions, let it go. Do what you can, and surrender the rest to the Invisible World. Now you are ready to move on to the last step.

7. *Read the signs that the Invisible World is sending you.* Pay attention to images, sensations, dreams, people, vibrations, and energies, and make sure you are receiving them at a high level of perception, such as in mediation or quiet contemplation. This higher level of awareness will send you a clear message about what you need to do next.

From here, you simply need to open your mind to the new reality. Continue to do what is within your control to manifest your reality, and then let it happen. Watch as the energy of the Invisible World works with your positive energy and brings you what you desire.

12

Our Collective Future:
Codes, Cycles, and World Events

For thousands of years, people have been going to prophets to hear about the future. In ancient Greece, political and military leaders would visit the Oracle at Delphi to hear what the High Priestess would tell them about military campaigns, upcoming elections, and other political affairs. The Priestess never said, "This will happen" or "That will happen"; she always answered questions simply, sometimes in what appeared to be a riddle. The interpretation of her answer was left up to the person asking the question.

Major world events can be predicted based on calculations because the universal forces apply to all of us collectively. If we calculate the date of the fall of the Berlin Wall

(11/9/1989), we discover it happened on a day that had the energy of 11, a day of higher vibration, when the Universe supported this incredible act of freedom. America asserted its independence from England when the Declaration of Independence was adopted on 7/4/1776, a day with an energy of 5, which is the energy of freedom.

If we work against the universal energy, we will struggle. By attacking Iraq on a date that had the energy of 1 (3/19/2004), the United States set itself up for a long, protracted war, because projects begun at a time with the energy of 1 are long-lasting. I predict that the war will last to at least 2008 and perhaps as long as 2012.

One of the most dramatic recent events was the tragedy of September 11, which was forecasted by the Mayan calendar and the walls of the Great Pyramid of Giza. There are two books about the prediction of the September 11 tragedy, based on the calculations made on the walls of the Great Pyramid of Giza and the Mayan calendar: *Beyond Prophecies and Predictions* by Moira Timms (Ballantine, 1993); and *Our Origin and Destiny* by Kathy L. Callahan, Ph.D. (A.R.E. Press, 1996). Astrology shows us that the attacks on the World Trade Center happened right after we entered the Era of Aquarius (also known as the Era of Enlightenment), which is the 11th house, ruled by Uranus and characterized by sudden changes and discoveries. During this era, which will last about two thousand years, we will move to a higher level of perception. Events will wake us up, bring us together, and push us to attain this elevated perception.

As a master number, 11 is associated with higher levels of being, and these events provided us with an opportunity to rise to a higher level of understanding. The attacks, which happened on the 11th, have many 11s associated with them.

✳ The twin towers formed an "11" in the sky.

✳ New York was the 11th state to join the United States.

✳ The first airplane to hit the towers was Flight 11. It carried 92 passengers: 9 + 2 = 11.

✳ The second airplane to hit the towers carried 65 passengers: 6 + 5 = 11.

✳ The total number of passengers in all four flights (two that hit the World Trade Center, one that crashed in Pennsylvania, and one that hit the Pentagon) was 254: 2 + 5 + 4 = 11.

✳ September 11 is the 254th day of the year: 2 + 5 + 4 = 11. There were 111 days left to the end of the year.

* The name "George W. Bush" has 11 letters.

* In America, the phone number we call in an emergency is 911: 9 + 1 + 1 = 11.

* "Afghanistan" has 11 letters.

* President Bush announced "mission accomplished" after the fall of Iraq on 5/1/2003, a date which is an 11.

* The tragic train bombing in Madrid happened on 3/11/2004—another 11. It happened 911 days after September 11, 2001.

The Pyramid at Giza: The Writing on the Wall

The tragic events of 9/11/2001 were predicted on the walls of the Pyramid of Giza and also by Nostradamus. In fact, on the King's Chamber of the Pyramid of Giza, we can find many historic dates, such as August 1914, November 1918, May 1928, September 1936, March 1945, August 1945, and August 1953.

The King's Chamber represents the victory of wisdom over ignorance. The dates between August 1914 and August 1945 point toward the first and second world wars. August 1945 is the date the atomic bomb was dropped on Hiroshima. August 1953 marks the end of the Korean War and the discovery of DNA. And the date

September 17, 2001, is on the walls of the Pyramid as the sixth day after the heavy Storm—a day on which we woke up with different eyes after suffering a global calamity. This day, September 17, 2001, has also been identified by the Mayan Calendar as the day that is six days after the "Big Storm."

Solaris: The New Era of Light

According to the prophecies, we are reaching the end of the current cycle, which is the ending of the Era of Pisces. We are also nearing the end of the Era of Iron (Kaly yuga), which has lasted the past two thousand years. Many of the predictions that have been made by the great prophets are now ending. We are entering a new age of light, the Era of Solaris. In this age, we will acknowledge who we are and what we need, and we will no longer be afraid of looking at the future.

The Mayan calendar identifies that the current cycle of history will end in 2012. The Bible also predicts the end of a cycle in 2012. The Great Pyramid starts its predictions in 3999 B.C. and ends them on March 21, 2141.

Because so many of the predictions and prophecies we've read or heard throughout history are of negative or catastrophic events, we are often afraid of predictions. We are afraid of the power of our own minds, and we often don't want to know what is ahead. But if we don't acknowledge who we are or what our potential is, we can't manifest the future we desire.

Ultimately these changes that were predicted thousands of years ago and the ones yet to come offer us the opportunity to raise our collective consciousness to a much higher level in order to bring in the Era of Light.

EPILOGUE
MY PREDICTIONS FOR A BETTER WORLD

I would like to end with my own predictions for the world and my beliefs about how things will change for the better.

There is an incredible collective power created when people work together to create good in the world. After the attacks on the World Trade Center, which was possibly one of the most horrific examples of evil and negativity many of us have ever experienced, the people of New York City and the entire country pulled together in countless ways. Through prayer, volunteer work, fund-raising, grief-counseling groups, and support for the merchants whose businesses were suffering, people became much more open in relating to one another, which had a tremendous healing power.

Throughout history, in the face of evil and adversity, the beauty of the human spirit has shone through again and again. A large group of people working together can manifest peace on earth because the Universe will support our efforts.

Now that we have entered the Age of Aquarius, there is a new awareness, a new frequency, and a new order in the Universe. We are heading into a future world where we will all manifest our light and loving intention.

I have many significant predictions for the next thirty to one thousand years. My predictions are based on many of the calculations previously mentioned and on reinterpretations of some of the predictions made centuries ago, as well as on my own visions. I believe I am a vehicle to reveal important events, some of which we can prevent from happening.

If you find any of these predictions upsetting, remember that they are future probabilities based on where we are at this time. The future is not fixed. If we all work for the good of the world, we will see big results. Many prophecies have spoken of dramatic changes that will be brought about by melting polar ice caps, as if this were an inevitability. But this prediction, like others, can be shifted by the unified focus of our collective mind. Collectively, we will figure out a way to prevent the catastrophe of melting ice caps. We won't sink. Our civilization will survive—if we all choose with our hearts the greatest good.

* We will eradicate diseases such as cancer and AIDS, MS, and diabetes. There will be amazing discoveries involving DNA and huge technological advances in the medical field.

* We will start cloning babies after 2020 as a regular procedure. Families will want designed babies and perfect children that are free from genetic mistakes and illnesses. This is the beginning of a much longer life on earth.

* We will reverse the aging process by creating anti-gravity devices. As a result, the life span on earth will increase from 126 years to 180, to 240, and to 370 in the next five hundred years. During Dvapara Yuga we will live for one thousand years.

* We will discover a speed of light greater than the current one. As a result, we will travel into space, collectively at first and then individually. We will have our own spacecraft, much like we have our own cars now. Our own individual airplanes will differ in shape from the ones we know today.

* Healing the body will be instantaneous. Using the new speed of light, the body will be healed by light therapy because the body is a "frozen" beam of light. Healing will include putting the body into a tube with very high light frequencies that will instantly restore the right energies in the physical body and bring the body back to natural health.

* We will connect with civilizations from other galaxies with other levels of evolution and discover new planets, new galaxies, and new forms of life.

* We will resolve the mysteries of who we are, including the central mystery of the process of life and death. We will understand the mystery of death and be able to connect with people in spirit form outside the world of physical matter through special frequencies in the electromagnetic field.

* In a frame of thirty to 120 years, humanity will relocate on Mars and on a new planet located in a new galaxy called Allandra.

* In the next seven to eighteen years, female energy will be dominant, and female spiritual leaders will rise in power.

* The stock market will fluctuate, and there will be no improvement in the economy in the next ten years.

✳ The year 2007 will bring some major shifts in thinking in America, which will prepare the United States in 2008 for the most interesting election in history. Vice President Dick Cheney will have heart trouble, which will cause President Bush to replace him with Condoleezza Rice, setting her up to run for president in 2008, although it may be another Republican woman who gets the nomination. Rice (11/14/1954) will be in a personal year 8, which is a very good personal year to run for president, but not nearly as good as a personal year 1. For Hillary Rodham Clinton (10/26/1947), it will be a personal year 1. Altogether there will be three women running for president.

✳ The culture war in the United States and the clash between cultures and belief systems of the West and the Middle East will continue for a while. All the predictions talk about Armageddon, the final battle of good and evil. Most people don't realize that Armageddon is a mountain in Israel. If the clash between the Middle Eastern traditionalists and the West continues, the biblical prediction of Armageddon will occur. (This does not mean we have to despair. As humans, we have free will. We can turn things around, and the energy of the Universe is very much with us at this crossroads.)

* There will be a shift in beliefs and consciousness from 2007 to 2012. Every current Middle Eastern leader will be replaced, and it will happen quickly. There will be war in the Middle East, but it will not wipe out mankind.

* There will be no nuclear war on earth. If a nuclear bomb is launched, it will be against Israel, but it will not lead to a nuclear war.

* There will be no terrorist attacks in the United States in the next seven years.

* Several comets will come close to Earth in 2007, 2027, 2063, and 2092.

* As part of the shifts and changes in the world, the United Nations will change the way it works. In the next four to fifteen years, Europe, Asia, and America will find more unity.

* In the next thirty years, the world will have one monetary form. The world will have more financial unity by 2020 or 2030. We will not have paper money and banks.

* All over the world, there will be an end to monarchy, the papacy, and the presidency. In the United States, there will be no government as we know it. These systems will no longer be needed on earth in a time frame

of fifty years. This will bring more equilibrium, peace, and stability among humans.

* After 2012, the standard laws of life on earth will start to change. More human rights will be incorporated, changing the Constitution of the United States. This will change the way we relate to each other. There will be more brotherhood and more caring for each other. We will be trying to heal our collective karma from the past two thousand years.

* In America, there will be major changes to the laws and to the Constitution in the next eight to eighteen years.

* The new generations (after 2012) will return to nature and to our spiritual origins. They will also return to a clear sense of right and wrong, calmness, and mental stability.

* After 2012, humanity will unite around one religion and come together in one spiritual brotherhood under the same God.

* Around 2023, a new negative leader will emerge from the Asian world, preaching negative issues.

* As a result of global warming, major changes to the earth will take place in the next seven to 120 years, including more natural disasters such as earthquakes,

hurricanes, tornados, and high winds. More hurricanes, worse than ever before, will hit different parts of the United States, and there will be major earthquakes in Japan, Europe, and California in the next two to twelve years.

* The seasons on earth will change. In parts of the world where we once had four seasons, we will have only one season (for example, only winter or only summer), depending on the geographical location.

* In 2012, there will be another "Big Storm." This will have to do with a major shift in our awareness and with realizing that we're in the process of warming the planet and facing the danger of sinking under water.

* Already, as has been predicted, the average temperature has risen twelve degrees in the North Pole and eight degrees in Alaska in the past few decades. If the process of global warming is not resolved in the next fifty-five to 125 years, major parts of the world (everything close to the North and South Poles) will disappear under water around 2141. This will be a world-changing event. The year 2141 is the end of a great cycle, according to the Mayan calendar and the Great Pyramid. However, humanity will survive, as it always has.

* The new Messiah was born on Easter 2000. When he becomes thirty-three years old, he will be the same age that Jesus was when he died. He will pick up where Jesus left off with a mission to help us one more time. He will reveal himself in 2033, the end of the transition from the Era of Pisces to the Era of Aquarius, which is the Era of Light known also as Solaris.

* Peace will prevail on earth from 2100.

* Realizing we must make major changes, people will shift their minds and their behavior, and politicians will not be the only major influence on popular thinking.

Knowing that the Universe supports us, we must each be committed to breaking the stale habits and conditioning and opening up to new ways of thinking, believing, and relating to each other. We live in a time of Awakening. We can choose to evolve—as the code of the Universe is pushing us to do—or we can resist growth and change. But the more we can accept that change is the dynamic of being alive, the easier it will be to transform and move our human family forward, out of the shadows of fear and into the Light of Love that was meant to be.